DORO

DORO

Doro Ģoumãñęh
and Brendan Woodhouse

unbound

First published in 2023

Unbound
c/o TC Group, 6th Floor King's House, 9–10 Haymarket,
London SW1Y 4BP
www.unbound.com

© Doro Goumãñẹh and Brendan Woodhouse, 2023
Maps © ML Design, 2023

This book is a work of non-fiction based on the life, experiences
and recollections of Doro Goumãñẹh and Brendan Woodhouse.
The authors have stated to the publishers that, except in such
minor respects, not affecting the substantial accuracy of the work,
the contents of this book are true.

Text design by Jouve

A CIP record for this book is available from the British Library

ISBN 978-1-80018-255-4 (hardback)
ISBN 978-1-80018-256-1 (ebook)

Printed in Great Britain by Clays Ltd, Elcograf S.p.A.

1 3 5 7 9 8 6 4 2

This book is dedicated to the ever-rising number of people who did not make it. To the people who drowned in our sea, to those who fell in the desert, to those who died in the torture camps, who died in the cold streets of Europe, who committed suicide; those for whom European politicians wrote policies, knowing full well that it meant painful and lonely deaths for those who dared seek sanctuary in our lands. It is especially for Ibrahim, Adam and the 117 people who drowned on 18 January 2019.

This book is also dedicated to the creators and enforcers of our hostile environment, which punishes refugees for just trying to survive. We see through you. Through your fake sympathies, through your lies and contempt and willingness to sacrifice people and principles and, in fact, anything or anyone in your desperate claw for power. We see your racism too, for you would have stopped all of this if the people that were coming were white.

Contents

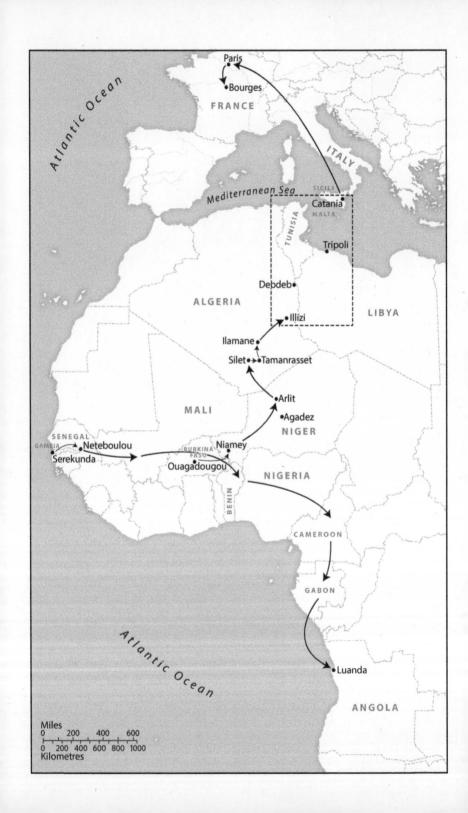

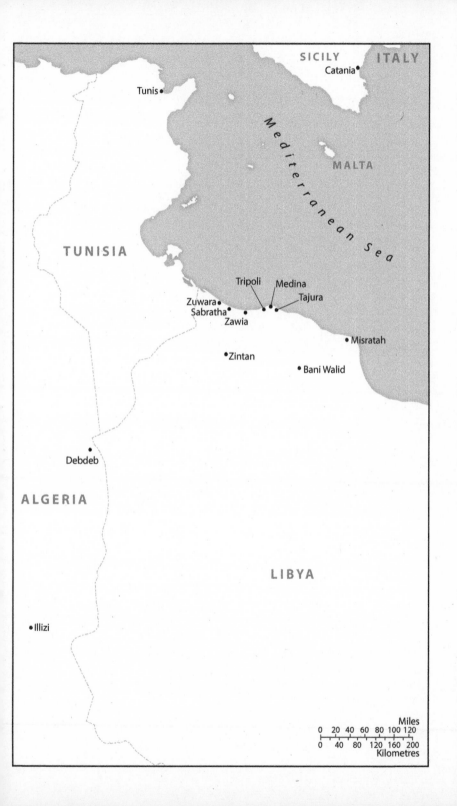

SICILY   ITALY
                Catania•

Tunis•

                                    M e d i t e r r a n e a n   S e a

                                         MALTA

TUNISIA

                          Tripoli   Medina
                    Zuwara•   • • •Tajura
                 Sabratha• Zawia
                                                    •Misrath
                          •Zintan
                                         •Bani Walid

            •Debdeb

ALGERIA

                                         LIBYA

   •Illizi

                                              Miles
                                    0 20 40 60 80 100 120
                                    0   40 80 120 160 200
                                              Kilometres

Prologue

This is Doro and he is beautiful.

Believe me when I say it. He is beautiful. His inner strength is humbling, and it shines through anything that your eyes may see. He is kind, generous, thoughtful and gentle, but his story should chill us to our bones because Doro has suffered for his dreams more than I could possibly describe. When I hear people say 'send them back', I think of Doro and others like him. This gentle man, who is now a dear friend of mine. They're talking about him.

I said to him, when he asked me to help him write his story, that not everyone will be kind. That people will make hateful comments. I said I'm sorry that some people will say that he is not welcome. 'Don't blame them,' he said, 'they have never suffered like this.' His human understanding and forgiveness are deeply affecting to witness. If only they knew. If only they could spend time with Doro, then some of his empathy might rub off on them.

Doro

I was one of the people who helped rescue Doro, from a small, blue rubber dinghy, trying to escape from Libya and make it to Europe. It was an encounter that will stay in my mind for ever. I didn't know that we'd become friends. I didn't know what had happened to him. And I didn't know that a year later I'd be helping him to write his incredible story. All I knew was that there was a boat, a small boat, moving slowly through the waves. That people were on it, and unless they were helped, then, in all likelihood, they would drown. And nobody – nobody – deserves to drown at sea.

Against all the odds, Doro survived, not just the rescue but the ordeal that led to him even being there, and he is alive to tell his story. That is not the mystery, and I don't want people to read this as a story about some victim. He is more than that. He is more than a survivor. This is a story about a champion, a hero if you like, and that is a term that I don't use lightly. Nevertheless, there are difficult questions ahead; how will Europe welcome him? Will he be granted asylum, or will he end up being sent back home? Will you think that he's a refugee or an economic migrant, and after reading this, will you care? Could you be the one to simply send him back? Or do we all need to think a little differently? Listening to people like Doro and seeing their suffering at first hand has certainly changed my perspective. Maybe it would for you too? Can you answer what exactly distinguishes a refugee from an economic migrant? Why are some people accepted, yet others aren't? Is the reality truly so black and white, or are there many shades of grey? There is certainly a distinction between how our governments set policies for welcoming refugees from different parts of the world. These policies seem particularly detrimental to those from African nations.

My name is Brendan. This is not my story.

Prologue

I want to tell you about Doro, but in fact I'm going to let him tell you. I'll come in from time to time with an explanation or with something that I saw, but most of this will be Doro speaking. It's his book, and his words will be in a different typeface from mine, so you can see when it's him speaking.

I am a firefighter in the UK and in my spare time, I sometimes do voluntary search and rescue work in the Mediterranean Sea. I've taken part in ten search and rescue missions, both in the Mediterranean Sea and on the shores of Lesvos, in Greece. I have taken part in the rescue of over 8,000 people and in doing so I've witnessed and been unable to stop the drowning of hundreds of people who try to make it to Europe. Since 2014, over 24,000 people have drowned in the Mediterranean Sea,* including over 5,000 children. This horrific, ever-growing death toll is what drives me to campaign for refugee rights, compelled by the unacceptable injustice of policies that appear to deliberately exploit death by drowning as a deterrent to those who have the audacity to seek sanctuary in our lands.

I've seen a lot of things in this time, and I've met a lot of incredible people, although I've never met anyone who has experienced as much as Doro and is still able to talk about it, who still wants to talk about it and is still so humble, so kind. How he has survived is beyond me, but he has done more than just survive. He has helped others along the way and maintained his empathy and love for other people despite every hardship that he has endured. I want to tell you Doro's story, but it is perhaps important to first talk about what Sea-Watch is, who the crew were, and why we were there to meet Doro and the others in the first place.

* UNHCR (the UN refugee agency) data portal, https://data.unhcr.org/en/situations/mediterranean

3

Doro

Sea-Watch is an NGO (non-governmental organisation) which was originally formed to observe human rights abuses and failures of European border policy, but it quickly had to adapt to becoming more of a search and rescue organisation. In 2014/15, a fleet of European naval and coastguard vessels was deployed in the Central Mediterranean in what was called Operation Mare-Nostrum. There had been massive loss of life and it was clear that what was being done was simply insufficient. In 2015, Sea-Watch bought its first ship and started operations, sending its small vessel into the unknown. Over the next few years, Sea-Watch has improved its operations, purchasing new ships, developing crew training, and even getting planes into the skies above the sea in order to observe and spot for boats in distress, and in doing so, it has helped save thousands of people. In that time, Europe has changed its policy, withdrawing its assets.

It was the beginning of January 2019 and I had arrived in Malta ready to start a four-week mission as I had done many times before, although this time it was unusual because there were already rescued people on the ship. I'd been reading about them in the news: how they'd been rescued before Christmas but had been refused entry into Malta. The Maltese authorities had forced our ship *Sea-Watch 3* to wait outside their ports without offering a port of safety to the people that the previous crew had rescued. It was becoming a worryingly common development in human rights on our borders that the authorities thought it appropriate to effectively close their doors on human beings seeking sanctuary. It brought concerns over what would happen when they finally allowed us to bring the people to shore. We didn't know if our ship would be confiscated, or if we would be criminalised – as had been the case previously with other rescue ships.

Eventually, Malta agreed that they would let the crew on the ship exchange places with a new crew and we were ferried out to sea to swap over with them. I wasn't aware of this happening before and it was unclear how the authorities would treat us at the time. Our main concern was for the welfare of the people on the ship who had escaped from Libya. We knew that many of them would have experienced torture and imprisonment. How would this effective captivity at sea affect them?

The most rapid handover between the old crew and the new crew had to be made and there simply wasn't time for the crews to properly pass information on. Then, as the handover was happening, one of the rescued people jumped from the ship in an attempt to swim to land, such was his desperation. He was quickly picked up by the crew and brought back onto the ship. Later, when we found out that he'd been tortured in a Libyan prison, it was clear why he felt such emotions at being kept locked up on a ship, so close to land. It was tough for them to see the old crew, friends as they had become, saying their goodbyes. Why were they allowed to land, and the rescued people not? Was this a trick? Would this new crew be taking them back to Libya? Anything seemed possible in the minds of people who had experienced so much trickery and dishonesty from smugglers, torturers and the many people who had exploited them in Libya. We did the changeover as quickly as we could, and with the old crew on their way back home, it was our job to take over from where they had left off.

In the first few days of my mission, instead of training to rescue people, as we would normally do, I had been teaching a baby to walk on the cold metal deck of the ship. I had played and drawn pictures with the children that were there and made friends with many of those who had been rescued and had been on the ship for two weeks already. It seemed barbaric to let people, especially children, suffer in this way, within sight of Europe. How our politicians could turn their backs on these kids is incomprehensible to me. They were left within sight of land for weeks before they were allowed to come to shore. It seemed unnecessary and cruel.

After a few more days, though, Malta made an agreement with other European countries that if it offered a port of safety to the people on our ship, then they must be taken elsewhere to other countries in Europe. It had just been a political game, with human beings being used as pawns between bickering politicians. Why they can't decide what to do with the people that get rescued is beyond me, but it certainly shouldn't be at the expense of the men, women, babies and children who were forced to sleep, play and live on the aft deck of our ship.

Eventually though, the Maltese coastguard boats came and took the people to shore. Happy faces smiled and waved at us as they went. They had been rescued on 22 December and spent Christmas Day and New Year on our ship. Meanwhile, the political leaders in charge of deciding to not offer them a safe port had gone to church on Christmas Day, had gone home to their families and believed that they were truly Christian. On 9 January the ordeal at sea was finally over. The next stage of uncertainty for them, and endless waiting, was about to start, and for us it was time to bond as a crew, get to know each other and train for the rest of our mission. We sailed away from Malta and into the open seas. Our destination would be what has become commonly known as a search and rescue zone, in international waters, just north of the Libyan coast.

Sea-Watch had been formed in 2014 by just ordinary people. A shopkeeper, a locksmith, a university lecturer, plus doctors and paramedics all clubbed together and formed this organisation from scratch, using donated money, as many people in Europe were aghast at the loss of life in our seas and felt compelled to do something about it. This way of ordinary people stepping forward to crew the ships as volunteers has been repeated on every mission that Sea-Watch has completed. This mission was no different. We are the civil fleet.

Kim, an instantly likeable, articulate Englishman with long dreadlocks flowing to the small of his back was the head of mission. He gathered us together to start the training which only lasted a short while, as many of us had been on missions before. Kim is well spoken, very patient and kind, with a perfect balance of humour and seriousness. He had been on one mission after another for months on end and is hugely experienced and respected. Despite all of that though, he carries no arrogance, treating first time volunteers with the same dignity and respect with which he would treat the ship's captain.

He set out the roles of the crew. I was to be driving one of the RHIBs (rigid-hulled inflatable boat) and had two Italian journalists in my crew: Bepe and Federico. It takes me a long time to trust journalists, but they were both approaching the whole subject with sensitivity and compassion. They clearly had the intention of reporting what was happening in a fair and dignified manner. Federico had been on boats before, but I had to spend quite a while teaching Bepe how to tie the knots, and what to do when he was on board. He carried a little piece of string with him everywhere he went so that he could practise. I liked his acceptance that he would be a crewmate first and a journalist second, but it would also be massively important to have good, responsible reporting from the ship, as without the photographs and news stories, nobody would know what is happening at sea, and nothing would change.

It is a difficult balance to get right, between accepting the need for the cameras and their inevitable intrusion on the privacy and dignity of those we rescued.

The other RHIB was being driven by Rob, who is probably one of the most caring people on the planet. He has spent a long time helping refugees, having first started volunteering in 2015, and then packing in his job in The Netherlands to do humanitarian work on a near full-time basis. He is charming and charismatic, with an uncanny resemblance to Will Ferrell, both in terms of his looks and his sharp sense of humour. He also had a photographer on the RHIB with him: Doug, an American photojournalist who I had first met in Lesvos, helping refugees in 2015.

We had a twenty-two-strong crew, including doctors, paramedics, deck hands, a bosun, engineers, a captain, officers, and the truly remarkable Anne, with the job title of 'guest coordinator'. Anne is from Amsterdam, and her job was to make sure that everybody we rescued was looked after, in terms of food, welfare, support and even entertainment; boredom can be a big negative factor if someone is confined to one room on the back of a ship for days on end. Anne was absolutely tireless, without a trace of selfishness and probably possessed the most robust work ethic out of any of us. It was reassuring to have her with us.

We sailed south towards Libya, not knowing if we would find people to rescue, and if we did, it was unclear what would happen if we brought them back to Malta or Italy. Political tensions were raised, and previous crews had been threatened by politicians for what they termed as 'facilitating illegal migration', but in truth, all we were doing was saving people from drowning as these same politicians proposed no rescue or reasonable other solution whatsoever.

Prologue

What is often forgotten in all the political commentary is that the people being rescued from this sea are real human beings, with brothers, sisters, parents and children. That they have real hopes, dreams and fears, and that these are as valid as yours and mine. Refugees, or migrants, or whatever you want to call them, are just as important and special as any one of us, and I am bewildered by the idea that the people on these boats are seen by some as unimportant or disposable. How have these attitudes become so mainstream? How are they even tolerated at all?

Over the last five or six years, I have taken part in dozens of rescues, meeting thousands of the people making this dangerous sea crossing. Each of them has a different story to tell, and in my time, I have heard countless individual accounts of what has happened to them and the reasons for them embarking on a journey which takes so many lives. I have decided that in those moments, whilst I am on a mission, it doesn't matter to me whether they are refugees or 'economic migrants' because nobody deserves to drown at sea. They deserve to be rescued.

Chapter 1

When Friends Meet

I was driving the RHIB towards a report of a rubber boat in distress. Wind was spraying water up from the bow and washing all over us. They had been seen by a humanitarian spotting plane, reporting up to fifty people on board. We were told its location and the direction in which it was travelling, but it was some distance from us. The *Sea-Watch 3* had dropped our RHIB in the water maybe an hour from its location, and we were going to their aid as fast as we could. Behind us, the *Sea-Watch 3* disappeared from the horizon, and I followed the coordinates on the GPS. Although we went about as quickly as humanly possible, we had to slow down from time to time to check our position as we were bouncing through the waves at such speed, for so long, it would be easy to go in the wrong direction.

A rubber boat would be all too easy to miss in these conditions, with the peak of a wave in the distance sometimes causing us to check false alarms.

A small dot on the horizon could be just a wave tricking our eyes, but as we got closer, I could see birds circling behind it. Just a fishing boat, chugging along slowly. I stopped to radio

the false alarm to the bridge on the *Sea-Watch 3*. Unbeliev-
ably, dolphins started leaping around us. They had been
following the trawler, enjoying the fish and movement of the
sea. It was a good sign, but there was no time to admire their
athleticism. No time to spare at all. The boat that we were
looking for could be in any condition. I've been there before
when we were too late. These horror shows that we've seen
with bodies floating in the water strengthened our determination to find them safe. We just kept going, hoping against
hope that we'd get there in time. I looked up, and there it was.
Another small dot, just below the horizon. I radioed to the *Sea-
Watch 3* about the potential spot and that we were going to
check it out.

The closer we got, the more obvious it became that this was
it. The blueness of the rubber boat contrasted against the
greyness of the sea. Silhouettes of human beings, soon to be
friends, stood out against the waves. Each person with their
own story to tell. Each one with their own reasons to be there.
All of them fleeing Libya, a place where so many people have
suffered the most incredible cruelty.

As we got closer to their flimsy little boat, Bepe was
crouched in front of the console, right at the bow of the boat,
trying to hold on to the ropes on the sponsons. Bepe was a
journalist on the ship but on the RHIB, everyone has to work.
I saw him trying to stand up and wave at the people. They
were all huddled together in the little blue rubber boat that
had brought them from Libya. He was waving his arm to the
frightened people on the boat. Few of them moved as they
cowered from us. They were terrified that we would be the
Libyans and that we'd take them back. So many of them had
been caught and returned before.

'Europa!' Bepe shouted. 'We are from Europe.' One arm

from the rubber boat raised in the air, and suddenly it dawned on them. They were safe! All of them stood up at once waving their arms at us, calling out in joy. Their relief was palpable. Their ordeal was almost over. Their hell in Libya would be behind them soon. But first we had to calm them down, get lifejackets on them, and transport them to the ship.

'Everyone sit down, calm down,' called Bepe, 'you are safe now.' They were hugging each other, but still I had to work out how many people were on board, and if their boat was sinking, or if there were any medical emergencies. 'Who speaks English?' An arm was raised: 'Me.' 'What is your name?' 'My name is Ibrahim.' And so, it began. The communication to find out all the information that we needed as Bepe was talking to Ibrahim. This information is critical to understanding the seaworthiness of their boat, their medical conditions, and what resources we would need in order to help them.

At the back of the boat stood an enormous figure in a grey tracksuit, and it was clear to me straight away that he would be an important person for us. I could see how he was telling people what was happening as there is always a mix of languages and information being conveyed back and forth. He was asking people to be calm and to sit down, assisting in the rescue immediately. He'd be key to get onside, I could tell that in an instant. Little did I know how close Doro and I would become. So much so that a year later, we'd still be speaking almost every day. That he'd become a close friend. But there he was – Doro with his incredible understanding of situations, turning to the others to help them relax, and helping with the rescue, having the understanding that most of them did not speak English and that they would be desperate for that information to be communicated. He knew how terrified the others would be and how these translations would provide reassurance and assistance to improve the situation for us all.

First, each of the people received a lifejacket. Then we transferred the people to our ship, the *Sea-Watch 3*, which at the time was the only NGO ship in the search and rescue zone. I still find it amazing that people have the courage or desperation to set off on such a dangerous journey, on a flimsy rubber boat, in the cold and dark, without even a lifejacket to keep them safe. Thousands of people have died making this journey, but this enormous death toll acts as no deterrent whatsoever. There are some in Europe who think that if the rescue boats aren't there, then people will stop coming, but they were making the journey before any NGO was in that sea, and still they come. They come when there are no NGO ships, or if we are there. It makes little difference. The Mediterranean Sea is a mass grave for people escaping Libya. It's a grave for our humanity too. But this isn't just the story of how Europe threw away its humane values, subverted its own laws and outsourced its humanity. This is Doro's story.

Chapter 2

Bourges

After the rescue, I spoke to Doro on the *Sea-Watch 3*. We spent a lot of time talking. He told me some of his story. I was absolutely gobsmacked. Not because of what he said – some of his experiences were similar to what I'd heard before – but because despite all of his history, he'd kept such a joyful, bubbly charismatic personality. He was covered in scars, and each one came with a description of its creation, but Doro was full of life. His resilience completely staggered me. As he was retelling his story, I wanted to give him the reassurance that it was over now, but it was Doro who was assuring me, 'Don't worry Brendan, I'm OK.'

I wrote a snapshot of his story on my Facebook page. It was shared tens of thousands of times. I photographed his scars in what felt like a massive invasion of his privacy. 'I want people to know,' said Doro, as he started to share more and more of what had happened to him. When I took the photograph, which is also used for the cover of this book, Doro was looking all serious, reflecting the seriousness of what had happened to him. I said, 'Come on Doro, you're beautiful, the camera loves you!' He started to laugh and I took the photograph which, I feel, really captures his authentic charm and warmth. 'This is Doro and he is beautiful' was read to Doro before I posted it to check that he was happy with what I said. 'But I am not beautiful, Brendan,' he said. I told him that he was, that he had a brilliant smile and his inner kindness could be seen. 'OK, Brendan. Do it.'

The next morning, I woke from my sleeping bag, with Doro alongside me. He asked me if anyone had commented on his post. I knew already that it had gained a lot of traction, and opened up the Sea-Watch post, where they had also shared his story. Over the hum of the engine, and with people starting to wake up all around us, I read out what I had written. He listened intently. He spoke quietly from his blankets: 'Yes, yes Brendan, that's right.' I asked if he wanted to know what people had said. He smiled: 'Yes please Brendan, do it'. As I read, he asked me to say thank you to the hundreds of messages that he had received, and after a while he became tired and fell back to sleep.

When Doro next woke up, he called me over and asked me to sit down. He asked me to help him write his story properly, including everything that had happened to him. I was humbled that he wanted me to do this for him, but I said, 'I'm just a firefighter, Doro. I'm not a writer. If you want, I can get a journalist to speak to you, or a professional, once you're in Europe?' He told me that he didn't want to open his heart to just anyone. He insisted that I help him, even though I told him that others might do it better.

Later in this book, you will read about what happened both on the ship and later as he arrived in Italy, but after his arrival, when he was first taken to a processing centre, France agreed to take some of the forty-seven people that we had rescued.

Doro was one of them, so he was eventually flown into France and taken to a small town called Bourges, about a three-hour drive south from Paris. There, he was to start his application for asylum, scared and lonely, without his friends, but determined to build his life again. I spoke to him nearly every day at the time, concerned for his well-being. Over the phone, we recalled the moments on the ship over and over again, and Doro went on to tell me more and more about what had happened to him before we found him.

After many phone calls with Doro, and his remaining insistent that he wanted to only share his full story with me, I travelled to Bourges to keep interviewing him as best I could. On the outskirts of the town, near a market, I parked my rental car and called him.

'Hey buddy, I think I'm here.' I looked around to see if I could see him, with the air-conditioning blowing cool air in my face.

'Brendan, my friend, I'll be there in five minutes.' I got out of the car, stretching my back as I went. It was July, it was the middle of the day, and it was hot. There wasn't much of a buzz in the market, with only a few people coming out in the midday sun. Doro had been ages; I rang him again, and he replied: 'Yes Brendan, five minutes.' He'd said that nearly twenty minutes earlier. I was worried that I was in the wrong place. He texted me: 'I'm on the bus. Not long.' I looked for the bus stop, not knowing which direction he'd be coming from. Then, as I saw the bus pulling up, I saw Doro right at the front. His smile could barely fit inside. As we walked towards each other it felt surreal for us to be in an ordinary setting, together on dry land, after so much that we had experienced together at sea. An immediate embrace and then we stopped to pull apart to look at one another.

'Brendan, I have missed you,' he beamed.

'I've missed you too, pal!'

Doro had been in town spending some of what little money he had, making sure that he had food for me. I said that I'd head back to my hotel soon to unpack. He was having none of it: 'You will stay with me. My home is yours Brendan, please?' Overlooking a small lake, his modest, first-floor flat would be my home for the next week, and he'd told everyone I was coming. He insisted on cooking for me. I'd already eaten, but he didn't care. It was a little bit overwhelming as he wanted to treat me like royalty and was determined to take me to see everyone that he knew. At first, I didn't know what to make of it and spent the first few hours driving to see some of his friends, being welcomed like something that I know I'm not, but Doro just wanted to show his happiness and gratitude, even if I felt that it was unwarranted. Late in the evening we arrived home, exhausted. I asked him if he would like to start the interviews for his story.

'Tomorrow, Inshallah,' he said. It was time for bed.

The next day Doro wanted to take me to visit more friends in Bourges. They too were refugees or asylum seekers, from Senegal, The Gambia and Bangladesh. The shared accommodation was filled with people from all over the world who had travelled to France for various reasons. Music and laughter fell from each balcony as we piled into my rental car to drive back to the lake by Doro's flat. All afternoon we sat by the lake. I was getting the feeling that Doro didn't want to tell his story, and I certainly wasn't going to put any pressure on him. If he didn't want to relive those moments, then that was fine by me. That evening at his flat, he had cigarettes, I had beer. Maybe he guessed how I was trying to work out how to ask him if he wanted to do the interview because he came to me with some papers that he'd written.

Doro had been writing his story in French before I arrived – so that we could spend as much of our time together as possible without working. I turned on my voice recorder and he started to read his story in English. I took notes as he spoke, trying to draw up the chain of events which had led him to this moment.

Over the next few days, I interviewed Doro several times. Starting sequentially to get the gist of what had happened, and then to fill in the gaps, and eventually going through more of the specific details.

At times he cried. At times there were moments of silence, which were filled with pained contemplation. At other times we laughed. The interviews lasted all week, which must have been incredibly tough for Doro. He was reliving some of the worst moments of his life. I tried to split his interviews up, not going from one traumatic event to another as I didn't want Doro to break down in front of me, so when it got traumatic, when there was a break, I'd ask him about home, or we'd talk about our time on the ship. But this is important to state: I am not a counsellor, nor a writer. I'm just a friend, and a guy that drives speedboats, but Doro didn't want to open his heart to a journalist, or a writer that he didn't know. So, forgive me if this does not have the articulation of a poet. It is though, as raw, as authentic, and as honest as can be.

Chapter 3

My Name Is Doro. This Is My Story

Why they give me the name Doro? The name of Doro is from my grandfather. My mother used to tell me that the name means 'a gift given by God'. Because when I was born, everybody think that I wouldn't be long in the life, but I still continue to be in the life. The name signifies a diamond, a black diamond is living in the water, and the water is not the water of salt.

My grandfather was a big farmer, buying and selling goats. The village name is Neteboulou. The name means one village. It was part of Gambia before the colonisation. After the colonisation time, the village came inside of Senegal. It is there that my mother was born. And after, her father became a big rich man. He had sixteen children. After he died, they divided the property, but in their culture, the women don't get the same rights of passing, as they should be part of another family. Only the men divide the property. My mother lost out.

My mother was married to my father for twenty-two years. He was from The Gambia. His father's name was

Doro, like me. Years later, my mother born two boys and one girl. I was the second boy, called after my grandfather. My father was a fisherman, and became very successful, and built a big house in the second capital of Gambia, Serekunda. He was happy. My father, what I remember of him, always he used to tell me that I will be happy one day, because he want every one of his children to be like him and be a fisherboy. He used to tell us to just maintain that work, even if him die. We just should be proud to do that job. If we do that job, we will get something from that job. You know. It is the only job that he used to tell us. Before I was fishing, I just wanted to be with my father. I didn't feel the fishing much before. To be truthful, I just feel like I want to be with my father. He used to go to the fishing, and he used to come back to the home, and he used to explain to us how to go in the water.

He used to sing before he entered into the water. He learned us how to communicate with the fish and how to communicate with the Master of Water. So, in our language we know everything about the water and how to fish. He used to teach us how to speak to the water, because in the water there is an imaginary thing, because there are plenty things inside the water imaginary. So, he used to tell us how what is inside the water is not like what is out of the water. And also, something he said that he learned from his grandfather, that if you want to be safe inside the water, you need to sing it. Every time you enter into the water, you have to go fishing, you will sing it and you will never come back empty-handed. He learned me how to sing to the water. I can sing for you. After, the spirit from the water will catch you like a friend, and he will save you. It is what he made us to believe.

My father's boat was a wooden boat. It was green boat, and on the left-hand side it was the writing 'Mother Love', because his mother have only him. My father explained to me that somebody made that boat for him, and every time when we would go fishing, he come back and pay him. Sometimes I used to go in the fishing place, and he used to show me plenty things about food and about water, how to drive the boat and how to catch fish. At that time, I think I was at the age of eleven years old. So, I remember plenty things. It had an old Yamaha engine and every time my dad used to maintain it. My dad was like a mechanic. Every time before we come to the water, he used to maintain the boat, doing everything, and showing me how to do the bottles of fuel and help me put them inside the boat.

When we had money, we bought a bigger boat, and we have two boats. We used to fish plenty fish because we used to spend a week and plenty time in the sea. It is an African wood boat, only space for an engine at the back and space for the fuel. And inside it had three wooden planks. The first is where the man who used to drive the boat would stay. The second is where we put the things that we used to use to catch the fish and the third is where we used to put our things, and me, it is there that I used to sit and where I slept. I never believed that somebody will stay in the sea up until the night, even if the sea was calm and there was nothing that was floating. You will see the sky. It was blue and white. And up to the sky you will see those small white things. What do you call them?

The stars?

Yes, those stars and everything from there I know that there is God in this world, you know? It was my first day.

The first time that I was in the sea, I was eleven years old. I was dreaming plenty things. I was seeing plenty things. I dreamed that I was inside the sea. There was plenty things inside the water that I was dreaming. Plenty unimaginable things. In my dream, our boat was attacked by a fish. A big fish, making it rocking, and everybody died. I dream plenty things. So after then, I told my father and he know what to do. He go and talk to the old man in the village. He explained my dream to him, and it is from there that the old man does everything because of what I was dreaming.

There is one fish we call it a snake fish. He said we should catch him before we go back. And after when we go back, he will do the sacrifice with that fish. When my father come with that fish, he called the old man who know everything about water. He called him in the seaside and that man tell him to bring the fish. That old man called all the old people who stay in the beach side, and they sacrificed the fish. They cooked it with six kola nuts, three white and three red. After then they put in the corn. They put it on the food and cook with fish. They prayed and they talked. They prayed to God, so that they wouldn't get the accident that I was dreaming and said that it would be alright in the sea. After, they said that any time I will enter the water I will not have an accident. I was eleven years old, and I can remember like today.

It was one year before the accident of my dad. He came one day with him best friend and they carried the boat to his house and said that he wanted to go and sell fish in Mali. My dad said that to him friend. He packed the boat in the beach side. So, he went himself to Mali to sell the fish. It is there that my father died in a car accident. I was twelve years old; my brother was twenty-one and my sister was ten years old. I can remember as my father died and my mother collected us, we went to my uncles' house. Like my grandfather's village in Senegal. I spent in there up to ten years. By the time we reached in my uncles' place, my uncles were using me like a slave, because they carried their pickings. Their children were in the school. Their wives and me were going in to follow the goats into the bush. So, every day, when I was sent to follow the goats, I used to come back and leave the goats in the bush and come to the school place to see my friends and cousins. We were the same age. So, when they left the school, we started to play.

It was the early hours of the morning on the first day of interviewing Doro. On a small wooden table with three chairs we sat, with my microphone sat between us. A dim light lit the room with a haze of cigarette smoke clinging to the ceiling. It was good to be finally interviewing Doro, but I could see him getting tired from reading. It was time to ask him about home.
Tell me about the games you used to play.

I played football. There was one African game. People would sit down, and one would take something and turn round and put it in the back of someone.

I think that he is describing a game that we called Duck, Duck Goose.

Everybody will sit down in a circle and concentrate to the front. Nobody will look at your back. Somebody will get up and turn. They go all the way round and put the object in the back of you. If he comes round, he will touch you and he will not have the object. So we were playing. Always I liked that game, playing it with my friends. When he put it in your back, you will chase him round everybody, and before he reaches you sit down in your place. If he catches you, you will change places with him.

I also liked to play cards. That is my style. I played cards since I was small. I used to make my own cards from cartons. I would go and see the big people that were playing cards, and I would make a pack of cards from the cartons and draw on them the pictures with a pen. Then, I would call my friends and show them how the old people would play. Everybody played cards, and I always liked playing cards.

'Can you remember when I caught you cheating at cards, Doro?' Doro laughed a big toothy smile, and, in a moment, we were taken back to the ship. We'd been kept at sea for weeks before we were given a port of safety. We weren't allowed to just bring the people that we had rescued in to land. The regime of Matteo Salvini was desperate to criminalise humanitarian rescue workers and to simply stop anyone from seeking sanctuary in Italy. The mundane reality of our incarceration at sea was boredom.

The rear deck of the *Sea-Watch 3* had been turned into a dumping ground where the true values of our European governments could be seen for exactly what they are. Our forty-seven friends had escaped the most intolerable conditions in Libya and were in a very poor physical and mental state. Their scars ran deep through their skin and deeper though their minds. The relief that their ordeal in Libya was over was followed by the dismay of not being allowed to continue. Still for them, it wasn't finished. They were as we were: forced into a kind of purgatory, in a cruel waiting game orchestrated by politicians keen to deny any form of responsibility. We were told that the people weren't wanted – by anyone. But our ship was an oasis of love in a seemingly endless pit of abhorrent abandonment. We played games, told stories, cooked, and waited together for the petty politics to end, so that we could go to land.

I'd made a football, by wrapping an oily cloth in tape and I'd written 'FIFA' on it. They cleared the sleeping bags and blankets from the rear deck, and soon it was Wembley Stadium. All the troubles slipped away as the only focus was the ball, who to pass it to, and how to score past the skinny Sudanese man, standing between two coats, laid on the floor as goalposts. Football is amazing like that. Our differences and our problems in life are almost completely forgotten in those moments when all you have to think of is a game. In this temporary state, everything is transformed. Cultural, social and religious differences are meaningless to the ball, and the game becomes everything.

Rob, another crew member, had brought his ukulele and there was a guitar with a string missing. Sometimes you'd find Rob giving ukulele lessons. Other times, you could hear the sound of our broken guitar being played by one of the people that we had rescued. Mamadou would be making a song up. He couldn't play, but he'd be hitting the strings and making up his own tune. Music too, the great human connector, reducing boundaries and borders to being exactly what they are, just lines on a map. We can all play and listen together, enjoying our different styles, soaking up the enrichment of something new.

We had books too and did fitness classes. We even set up a cinema night with a laptop. We did everything we could to distract from the waiting game, which just seemed endless, and completely pointless. Unless the point was to keep these guys suffering? I think maybe it was. That's certainly what it felt like.

One of the best things we had to distract us all from the tedium was playing cards. I think we had about five or six decks of cards, and no matter where you went on the ship's rear decks, you'd find a few people sitting in a circle playing a game. Doro was the master, or so we thought, until I caught him cheating.

There we were, Ismael, Yassiry, Doro and I playing this game on the top bunk of one of the hospital beds. It was always the same game. Doro was the dealer and was giving everyone five cards. Dealing to himself, I caught him dealing from the bottom of the pack. 'Hey, Doro. I've caught you. Cheating!!!' He started to laugh. Ismael called him Zigzag, and the whole place was teasing him. Then the game was dealt, Doro dealing out the cards with a big smile, like nothing had happened, and nobody minded. His cheating was instantly forgiven and taken with humour. Nobody could be angry with Doro. He's such a kind, gracious guy, and he'd done so much for everyone already.

I sat there in the darkness looking at Doro, his mind skipping back to that moment – a huge smile appearing on his face – his kind eyes reflecting the TV screen which played in the background, lighting the room.

I remember in my own country in Gambia, I used to play cards. I know how to cheat at cards. I cheat well at cards. I understand cards very well, but I don't like gambling. Gambling is not something I like. I just like to play.

When I was young, I was very intelligent, but my uncles started to hurt me. I was facing beatings. I was facing hunger. When I was sent to look after the goats, I would come back and play with my cousins and my friends. And in the evening, when they came back, they would ask me 'Where are the goats?' The goats had already come home with their bellies full, but they would punish me for not watching them. Some of my uncles would punish me by not giving me any food. I would go to sleep hungry. Some of them would beat me up.

One day I was sitting in the front of the school, waiting for my cousins to come out of school, so that we can come to play. When I come home without the goats, my uncles used to punish me. No food throughout the day, closing me inside the room, no outside. One day I go back to the bush with the animals, and I leave the animals in the bush, and I go back and I sit down to the door of the school to wait for my friends and cousins to come out and go to play. That very day the teacher saw me in front of the school door and came and asked me my name: 'You, what is your name, my young?'

I responded in French; I'd never been to the French school but I had learned it. I responded, *'Je suis Doro.'*

'Why are you sitting every day in the school door?'

I just responded to him: 'All my friends and my uncles' children they are studying in the school, and me, I am going back to the bush. Only me to go and watch the goats. I cannot do that, which is why I come to the school to wait for my friends. We will go and play.'

'Do you like school?' asked the teacher.

I said, 'Yes, I was in school in Gambia before my father died, but when I come back to my uncles' village, no more school, they are treating me like a slave to go and follow the goats in the bush every time. And their children, they are in school.'

The teacher said, 'Welcome! I will talk to the principal.' So I entered the classroom. That is how I went to the school in Senegal. Nobody paid for me. Nobody registered me. I used to go to the school always with torn and dirty clothes until I got to grade five. After grade five, the principal used to buy my school clothes, not my family.

When I was small, the only thing that I was thinking was to revenge. But I didn't think to revenge as to hurt people. I want revenge to be an example to my uncles. You cannot birth children and throw them. You don't know tomorrow how they are going to be and who they are going to be. My direction to the French school was to be a big person in the school and I did it. When my cousins got home from school, they would go and learn from their books, in the house. But my uncles would call me and tell me to do small jobs in the house. Like they would call me and tell me to go give the goats water. After giving them water, the next job would come and then the next job, so I never got the chance to sit down to learn my books. But one thing that God gave me: every morning, I used to get up before everybody else and I'd learn my books. And I put everything in my head. In the school everyone was surprised. I used to always get better marks. My family were surprised how I was learning better than their children. I wasn't eating well. I didn't have the good clothes, and still getting better marks. They started noticing and liking me just a little bit. That's how I grew up. I never enjoyed the riches of my father.

Today I speak many languages. In Gambia I speak the

languages of Gambia, Senegal and all the tribes. I also speak French, English and Arabic.

I knew that Doro would be an important person to get onside, from the first time that I saw him on the RHIB, and on the ship this communication continued. Every day after the rescue, Kim would hold a morning briefing. He would talk about the position of the ship, where we'd been in the night and where we were going to. He'd ask if everyone was well, and he'd help talk through problems. Then Doro would communicate Kim's messages, first in French, and then into some African languages. Another translator would then finish off with the last couple of languages, but without Doro, this communication would have been much more difficult.

Doro wasn't just an interpreter on the ship though. For me, he was the litmus paper for the mood of everyone. He knew of every quarrel and disagreement, and smoothed things over as best he could. There's always going to be a disagreement when you force forty-seven people to live on top of each other like that, on a ship, through rough seas, in the middle of winter. Doro would listen to the others and act like a mentor, or guide, explaining to those who were scared that we'd take them back to Libya, that we would not. Or explaining to people at times that the wait would not be for ever. He'd been through the worst in Libya, and everyone knew it. They respected him and listened when he spoke. He spoke with kindness and empathy, and in conversations you could see him working his magic, making people laugh, or comforting them, or talking over what had happened to them in Libya.

He is a natural leader too, evident from the second I met him and from our first real conversation. After the rescue, and a short moment of celebration, the exhaustion hit the people that had been rescued. The deck was awash with people sleeping. Some had grabbed lifejackets to rest their heads on. Others just slept on the cold metal deck, as the ship rolled and tossed its way through the sea. Anne, our 'guest coordinator', had been making some rice with spices and beans to feed them, and soon a vat of food was ready, and we were waking people to eat the first food that some of them had eaten in days. After the meal, Doro saw our washing-up bowl, a large plastic laundry basket filled with plates. He gathered some of his friends and immediately, he was organising the others to collect the plates and help him wash the dishes.

'Come on,' he called, 'our rescuers will not wash our dishes', and straight away he was showing his humility, grace and respect, and helping the others to take part in looking after the ship. Later, I spoke to him to thank him for organising the dishwashing.

'Everybody must take responsibility on a ship,' he said.

Chapter 4

A Reason for Leaving

When I was twenty-two, I decided to go back to Gambia and be a fisherman, like my father was. I bring my family with me. I took my younger sister first and later my mom came to join us. It was before the time when I met my wife. I wanted to follow in my father's business. I started to do fishing. Some months later, I met one guy, his name is Joel. He is an Englishman that my father used to work with. He was getting the bosses and exporting the fish to other countries. After meeting that man in Gambia, we just visit each other and get work to do between him and me. We used our boat to catch the fish. We became big fisherman in the town. Sometimes he would bring three cars, and we became very well known. In 2011, I married my love, Awa Faty, and in the end of 2011, she became pregnant, and she born twins, but one died in childbirth. In 2014, she was pregnant again, but by then I had decided to start this journey. I never see my son; I start this journey.

After some time, the government decided to take the business from us. The president with his government decided to catch the fish. They buy boats to give to the fish-ermen. And everything come down. The business was trading the fish. We were making good money, and every-one was proud. Me, I depended on nothing, but people depended on me. I became a real fisherman and a real busi-nessman. In my main country Gambia, even the government recognised my business. And when the government decided to take over the business, it was a big disappointment. That was not our intention.

Some months later, we see in the sea plenty of new boats. Written on the boats was 'New Gambia'. I asked my friends: who are these boats? He said that they are the new government boats to fish and to sell. Then some friends heard that Joel was in prison, implicated by the govern-ment. They said that he was dealing drugs in the fish, but that was not true. He had just refused to do business with the government. That's why they lock him in the prison.

After a while, I hear nothing of my friend or his busi-ness. After the problem of that government, we could get nobody to sell the fish and my business closed. I was afraid. Everybody was afraid. Because when the business come down, the only thing is – we was afraid, me and my family – that they tried to put me in the jail. They tried to bring me problem. I lost everything but maybe I can lose my life. It's all about that, and people are afraid. Me, I didn't want to leave to go on this journey, I just wanted to leave and go to Senegal to stay there small time. Maybe when everything calm down, I go back.

The Gambia has a turbulent political history. It gained its inde-pendence in 1965, becoming a republic in 1970 and, until a military coup in 1994, was ostensibly a multi-party democracy, the longest running in Africa, with apparently freely contested elections every five years, though the People's Progressive Party (PPP) of President Dawda Jawara remained dominant for more than two decades.

After the coup in 1994, and a period of direct rule by the armed forces, a new constitution was approved by referendum, democratic elections were held, and Yahya Jammeh was elected president in 1996. Jammeh was in power for twenty-two years, a period of authoritarian rule with a painful record of extrajudicial killings, enforced disappearances and literal witch-hunts.

In 2016, a coalition of parties supported the opposition candidate, Adama Barrow, who was declared the winner of the election. After initially conceding defeat, Yahya Jammeh then reneged and refused to leave office. The Economic Community of West African States (ECOWAS) stepped in and Jammeh was forced into exile. A Truth, Reconciliation and Reparations Commission (TRRC) was set up, but many potential witnesses were too afraid to testify, some for fear of repercussions, since a lot of Jammeh loyalists were still in positions of authority, and others because of the requirement to recount and relive traumatic incidents in an open forum under the gaze of both the public and the live TV broadcast cameras.

The Barrow government has faced numerous difficulties and in December 2021 formed an alliance with the party of former President Jammeh, the Alliance for Patriotic Reorientation and Construction (APRC) – a move that shocked many.

But back to Doro's story in 2014.

I leave Gambia because I was afraid for my life. I leave the place because I fear. That was the problem. And my wife supported me to leave the place at that time, and my mom.

Nobody don't want to lose me. I was so young. And after my dad died, I was the one to look after the family and secure the family. When I lost my business, I lost plenty things. I lost investment. When you lose those things because of somebody, who suffers? It is your family. You will be panicked because you know that they have power over you. They will close your life. They will eliminate you. Nobody will know how you go. So it is better for me to be lost and people think I die for a few years after then, maybe I will come and communicate with my family, so that I do.

I moved first to Senegal. At that time, it was the secret agents, not the police officers who will come and find you. It was the secret agents. They will not put your name in a form. They will not put nothing. They will come and sit with your friends and chat with them, to know about you. Maybe one of your family people, you know, they will sit down with them. Some women, even – they used to see my wife when she went to the market. They used to see a man questioning. And my wife didn't even know those people. They will talk like they are my friend and pretend that they know me. At that time, I was in Senegal. I used to talk to my wife and my friends on the phone. They used to tell me all about that. They used to say that I should go away, I should run far from here, because by this time everything is very hard. They are always asking about you, the secret agents. So even my wife used to tell me, she's not a fool: 'What kind of people are those people?' So it is that what made me not want to go back.

Before I left, I went to see my mother. My mom told me, 'Before someone else make you disappear, make yourself disappear. When other people make you disappear, you will never come back.' So it is that time I go away. I said to her, 'I want to go far from this country, because my start was good, but it ended bad.' My mother explained to me that it was like my father. My father started, it was very good, but in the end he died. 'But you,' she said, 'I know you will make it. But be careful.' I then left home.

I cannot even go back and get lawyer and do justice. All those judges, they are in the hand of government. You can't do nothing. You don't have any power. So, the only thing I do and still I don't regret it, is to run. So that's why today I am here, and I am explaining you my life. And I am here today by the grace of God.

The only advice that my mother gave me is three things: be careful of others' property, don't steal from nobody and don't lie – and don't mind other people's business. Everywhere I go it is the first thing that comes in my brain: Don't steal from no one, don't lie, and don't put your mouth to other people's problems.

Doro had originally left The Gambia and moved to Senegal to escape the secret police and a potential 'disappearance'. He felt that he could not go back to The Gambia, but also felt that in neighbouring Senegal he was not safe from their clutches or even just the stigma of being a Gambian refugee in Senegal.

From there, I leave Senegal. The problem for me was I was fearing for my life even there. I was scared. And all of my family only caring about my life. Let me secure my life. The problem is, as long as you are in life, then you are there. And in that country people are seeing you and everybody know what is going on. So they will know also which kind of problem you have with the government.

People, they will always talk about that. I decided to go and start a journey. A big journey. A journey I never think it will be. The journey without nothing. No help. No brother and no father.

In my country plenty people go to Angola, making money and come back, doing business. So, before my whole experience, my intention was to go to Angola and work and have money. Before the time I was going to Angola, I didn't know this journey to Europe. I was going to Angola to hustle. I come from my country, but it was not to go to Europe.

At the time, the regime of Yahya Jammeh had ruled The Gambia with a strong arm. Political demonstrations and dissent were met with force and many people felt completely hopeless. Criminal networks used the country for smuggling illegal goods. Rents and businesses were stolen with government corruption at the heart of many of the peoples' issues. Nearly half of the people lived on less than $1.25 a day. There was little hope of finding a political solution for many people like Doro, and with Joel imprisoned, maybe he would be next. Yahya Jammeh had been president for two decades before Doro was forced to flee, fearing for his future.

He was not alone. In 2016, around 12,000 Gambians – a massive number for such a small nation – landed on the shores of Europe.

Chapter 5

The Start of a Journey

I start in Senegal to earn some money for two months. I was loading big trucks. The big Canyons, the trucks with rice and sugar. After getting small money, I started to continue my journey. From Senegal, I go to Mali. Mali is a very poor country and very dangerous. But it was so lucky for me that I had money because I worked in Senegal. I didn't take any time in Mali, and I passed through.

From Mali, I take the bus to Benin to go to Angola. From Benin to the border of Nigeria. From there we pass through Cameroon. And in Cameroon they will do the human trafficking and they will carry you in the night. They put you in the car and they will carry you to the forest and then you people will start to walk. In the morning you will sit doing things, and in the night you will start to walk. It is to cross the border of Cameroon to enter in Gabon. All that, we pass through the forest because the car drop us near to the border of Gabon. That place, I know that place very well. From the forest we used to pay people to show us the road, and we will buy our lights. We will buy our everything. Our food, we put it in the bag and start to walk. When it is daytime, we will stay one place in the forest. We will cook. We will eat. Until night started to come, and then we start to walk. After two days, we pass through the forest into Gabon, and we go to Luanda in Angola.

And in Angola there are plenty foreigners where you will lodge and go to work. I spend six months in Angola working hard. My intention was to stay in Angola to work, because before that time, Angola was getting plenty work. Masonry work, building houses. Plenty work, security. So before, when I was in Gambia, my aim it was to travel to any of the best country in Africa, so that I can make there. My intention was to stay in Angola for all months and years and to go back to my country and start my life. After Angola started to be hard, asking for papers, different papers, so me it was I say let me move from this place Angola, I hear this journey they explained to me; the journey to Libya to cross to go to Europe, so I followed those friends. They were telling me the money and I have it because I was working there six months. That's why I start this journey.

But when we are meeting people while we are travelling back, our money started to reduce. It is from there I went to Burkina Faso. In Burkina I was very lucky, but it was very poor also. I had to sleep in the street, and I found food in the rubbish. But one day I got a job in the grand garage of Burkina, called Rainbow garage. It was for tourist vans. I was a cleaner for these vans. It was nothing. I got another transport in the capital of Burkina, Ouagadougou.

Then we went to Niger. Niger was the hardest journey for me. Niger is poorer than everywhere. In Niger there is no clean water. Everyone is suffering because of the famine. I did not think that I could make it. In Niger I was sleeping in the street and starting to walk in the street to find work. Every day I see people working and I ask them if they need a worker or helper. One day when I wake up and I could see people building houses, and I went to them and said, 'My name is Doro, I have been in this place for one week. I have no food. Not good water. I've not washed my clothes. I've not even taken a bath. See how I'm dirty. I will work. I need you people to take me as a helper and I will work like you want. Even if I get a small salary for eating, it is good for me.' The place in Niger was Niamey, the capital. After the work in Niamey, I decided to pass to Algeria.

People have always moved. Human beings have migrated for as long as we have existed as a species. It is in our nature, as it is in the nature of nearly every single species of animal on the planet. We move around for a whole range of reasons. We always have done so, and we always will do. Not all of the people who migrate to Libya want to travel to Europe. Traditionally, and still today, many people travel to Libya to work, with the intention of sending money back home. People in the poorest African countries often travel to more affluent areas, like Angola or Libya, to take advantage of the better working conditions, currency and wages. In fact, many of the Asian refugees and migrants in Libya travelled there to work in the public service sector. Many of them end up in hell.

People from West and Central Africa have traditionally travelled to Libya to work and have done so for decades. East African smuggling networks operate in a different way to those migrating from West Africa, with gangs promising a new life far from home, often exploiting vulnerable communities from countries ravaged by war or famine, or affected by climatic changes. For each individual, though, the routes and the reasons for making it to Europe are different. It is impossible to look at a boat of people crossing the Mediterranean Sea and make accurate assumptions about where the people have come from and what the reasons are for their migration. There are too many myths and misunderstandings.

One thing is sure though: the mass displacement of people that we are seeing now is just the tip of the iceberg. Some of the consequences of the world heating up are food shortages and conflict, which can only worsen as regional conditions deteriorate. If you're worried now about mass migration and how we're dealing with it, then you need to consider what will happen if our political leaders do not create a rational and humane system for sharing the responsibility of these displacements.

The route that Doro took is not unusual. People often travel from their host countries to Agadez in Niger and then travel north either directly, through Sabha, or via Algeria. People from the East African countries usually take a slightly different route. Nearly every single one of the routes leads to a desert crossing at some point though, and the desert is deadly. It is impossible to know how many people have died trying to cross to Europe by sea, but the body count is already in the tens of thousands. At least some of the deaths are recorded, though many aren't. Few people have any idea at all, however, of how many are lost to the desert. As usual, we focus on what is immediately in front of us, with little understanding of what is happening on the way to Libya. Doro can describe what the people are facing far better than I can.

The Start of a Journey

We were sat opposite each other at his small second-hand dining table, gifted to him by a refugee charity. I read through what I had written. Doro rummaged through the papers of the story that he had written. We were connecting the parts of the story together, each time going over in detail what had happened before things started to go wrong. He didn't mind when I kept asking him for more and more information, but as the night went on, I could sense that he was starting to slow down. He translated to me what he had written in French, and then we'd go back over the details. It went on into the early hours of the morning, but Doro is resilient. He didn't want to stop for a break. He wanted to tell me about his time in the desert. This part of the journey, he felt, had been untold and for him, it covered some of the most important and impacting experiences of his journey.

Chapter 6

Desert From Niamey to Algeria

Niamey to Algeria took me three days. Many people had died on the way. In Niamey, I found work in building construction. I was doing masonry. As I worked there, I got money, and as I got money I went to the garage. That is one garage that has buses. And when I went there, I told them that I wanted to go to Agadez in Niger. As I got to Agadez, I saw plenty friends who are trying to get to Libya. Some were heading to Algeria. Some of them, I met them there. We knew each other on the roads. We met by working together to earn money. But most people that I knew on the roads in Agadez, they were heading directly to Libya. But I met some people that were heading to Algeria, as they didn't have enough money to go straight to Libya. To go directly to Libya from Niamey was plenty money. So, I followed the people that were going to Algeria.

As we go Arlit,* I meet again people there. It is from there

---

* A uranium mining town in Niger with a direct connection to the Tuareg rebellion of the 1990s and where Saddam Hussein allegedly tried to acquire uranium in the early 2000s.

they take the big trucks. They first take our loads. How they make the trucks: they bring the trucks, they put wooden planks in the front, middle and back, and tie all of our bags and food. And then they bring a cable, and you will climb the cable and find a seat on the truck. Me, I was in the front behind the cabin, facing backwards. But I was sitting on my legs. My legs were tired. You cannot move. People are plenty, and the loads, they are plenty. When you sit down, that is how you will stay until you reach where you are going. When some people got off, they collapsed, and their legs got problems and they could not walk. It is a hard journey. They drove us from the morning until around six or seven at night. If anybody falls off the truck, the truck will leave them in the desert, and they will die. Fortunately, nobody fell off our truck. Where they dropped us is then 200 km from Zintan. So we had to walk all of that way in the desert. It was one day on the truck and two days walking.

When your water finishes you die. It is like a soldier's journey. I saw plenty of people die. Some people, their water finished. They had food, but you cannot eat food without water. They sit down to wait for help, and it is there that they will remain. Some people, they walk until they fall down, and it is there that they will remain, because it is the desert, and it is hot. And nobody will help them. You cannot help them because you cannot help yourself. Like if you had a bag, you will walk until you throw your bag. Because the bag will be heavy in the desert. You walk with your shoe, if it hurts you will throw it because it will make you heavy. So in the desert you cannot help no one. If you like to help someone, you can't. You will die if you help. Of the people that I did not help,

I am 100 per cent sure that they would not make it alive to the city, because the distance was too far.

I wanted to know how Doro felt about leaving people in the desert. People are forced to make tough decisions in those kinds of situations, decisions that, fortunately, I've never had to make. It seemed cruel to push Doro on this aspect of his journey and it was way into the early hours of the morning. Doro was tired. He lit a final cigarette of the day and there was a silence as he contemplated what he had experienced. I could see his eyes change focus as he searched his memory for what had happened.

Of course, sometimes I feel guilty about those that we left behind. But we were so tired. Sometimes I think of the desert in Libya. But in the journey to Algeria, I never feel guilty. I was walking because I was so sure that I would reach where I was going. It was my first experience as a man. I threw everything away. My bag, my food and everything.

I saw lots of people in the desert that were dead. There was one convoy who started before us. As we reached this place, it was the hottest place. We walked until the night, and everybody dropped everything and went to sleep. We get up in the morning and walk again. Before 2 p.m., we started to see bags that they had thrown, and shoes. Some of us searched the bags for food and water, but there was no water. We walked another hour and started to see dead bodies. Me, I saw one woman in the sand, and I started to remove the sand from her with my hand. But the sand was covering her, and she was dead. I saw on her back she had a baby, and they were both being covered by the sand.

They were both dead. And the sand covered them like a blanket. And when I brushed the sand away, I saw the baby. I am sure that they had not been there long. We saw them soon after they had died. They died maybe a few hours before we came.

There are plenty of dead bodies in that place. Everywhere! In that place it is mind your own and mind your business. Everybody is going. Some people they got tired and sat down. We go. Some people they are with us, and they change the journey, and we leave them and follow the route. By the time we got there, we had split into many groups on the way. The people that came to Algeria in my group were not more than twelve.* Our group was composited of Nigerians and Gambians. When people were relaxing because they were tired, we left them. We were the first. Some people got up and followed us and some people stayed down. We always said, 'Let us walk, let's keep going, it is not so far now, let's go small, small.' And it was like that until we got to Silet, the first place in Algeria. After Silet we go to Tamanrasset.†

It is a bad road. It is worse than the sea. In the sea, you will die only, but in the desert, you will suffer before you die. The sun is hot. There is nowhere to escape it. No shade anywhere. Everywhere is hot. Our crew was two convoy, each taking seventy-eight people. That's how much. That's 156 people. My friend, the desert killed more than a hundred people. I will not forget that day. I entered into Algeria only with the clothes that I was wearing on

* In number.
† A high-altitude oasis city and stronghold of the Algerian Tuareg, Tamanrasset has a centuries-long trading history.

Desert From Niamey to Algeria

my back. Without nothing! After when I reached Algeria, I took off my shoes, my leg was getting big. We reached Silet. Some people had took off their shoes, but I had kept mine. We carry some of them in the hospital and give them water. They were suffering.

The desert is harder than the water, my friend. That's why sometimes I didn't want to explain the desert to you on the ship. In the desert, you will march until the night. You will not see nothing. Only the desert, my friend. No food. No drink. Nobody to come and help you. And the most bad things we pass were in the desert. Sometimes we march. The soldiers they will pass us. Some of us get luck like that. Like we, in my group. When we were marching, the soldiers who passed us gave us water and called the police officers to come and make an intervention. That time plenty people were tired. Plenty people had died. This journey was killing people. I wish even my enemy will not pass this journey.

They just told us when we march small, we will see the city. We don't know the roads. We are in the desert. You don't get any choice. But you pay your money, it's your power. But they drop you in the desert and they say you will walk. Only maybe one hour you will see the city. And I asked them, 'Why you people cannot carry us in the city?' They said it is trafficking. When they come in the city the police officers see them, they will lock them. The drivers dropped us in the desert. They are from Niger. They are the ones doing the trafficking. Some people march and die. Some people march and make it. It is just luck!

What kind of people make it? What kind of people don't make it?

49

I saw plenty of mysterious things. People getting tired and telling the others to go, and they will stay, and they will never come again. It was the women, because they were tired, and they cannot do nothing. It was the old who could not keep going. Like I say, one woman with her children on her back. She was not in our crew. We just see them lying dead. It was another convoy. The wind pushed the desert over them. Small parts of them were covered. They are lying down. They are already dead. The desert is covering them. And we see plenty people. And we see plenty bags in the road. Like us. We carry our bags until we drop when we are tired. The people who are in front of us. The people who are not making it are the people who in a small time will need water and food. In the desert they cannot make it. More women did not make it, but some women they make it. Some children also – they didn't make it.

After we get closer to the city the smuggler arranged for taxi to come and get us and will gather us together and give us advice. They said, 'If you go in the city, they will arrest us and take us to jail. Where are you going?' We said, 'Tamanrasset.' He said, 'OK, you people get in the taxi, we will drop you in Tamanrasset. Police officers will not see you people. So after, you people you will pay us.' When you agree, you enter into the taxi, and they take you to Tamanrasset and they will sell you. How they will sell you is they will carry you to another address, another house. They give you to the Arab man who demands money from them. They are dealing with blacks. You meet there plenty blacks. Bigger than you. They eat more than you. They are guarding the house. You cannot escape until you pay the money. It is the deal. That business is running before Libya. In Algeria itself.

What happens if you don't get the money? (Doro laughed as if I had missed the obvious.)

You will get the money. They will treat you.* They will beat you. They will make a phone call. They will tie you. They will do bad things. You must pay the money. I paid them 10,000 Algerians. I spent there three days and I paid the boss. It's about eighty euros. But I was lucky.

When I reached Tamanrasset, I was passing the police of Tamanrasset and they stopped to ask me where I come from and where I am going. Where are my documents? I admitted I had come the illegal way, so they took me to the police station. After two days they took me to the justice in Algeria in Tamanrasset. When I went to the justice, the justice asked me two questions: Why do you leave your country and why you enter our country without no legal way? I explained to the justice my story. And the justice of Algeria released me and gave me my freedom. He gave me a visa for two years to work in Algeria. I didn't expect this, and I thought I was so lucky. I expect to sleep in jail. It is in Algeria where I meet Ibrahim!

How Doro crossed this desert is a story that the rescue workers often hear. He speaks of himself as being lucky to have made it. I think that his view of luck is very different to most other people's perspectives though. To cross the desert, dry-mouthed, unable to sweat, muscles aching, and head throbbing is not my idea of being lucky, but Doro saw those who fell around him. His experience of the desert is from a perspective that I feel lucky not to have known, but his thoughts are with

* When Doro says 'treat you', he is referring to torture, or treatment.

the men and women that he saw laid dead in the desert all around him. Discovering this particular woman and child, with the desert slowly covering them in a blanket of sand, affected Doro deeply. As he explained how he found them, I could see him visualising his experience of that exact moment, putting himself right in that place in the desert as he tenderly stroked sand from her imagined cheek with the back of his hand. As he kneeled down and leaned forwards, it was like she was right there in front of him. His eyes filled as his voice softened; exasperated by the futility of her death, he spoke of her like she was the most important person in the world. And to somebody, she was.

Chapter 7

My Best Friend

The next day, Doro took me to meet some friends in Vierzon. Six of the other forty-seven people that we'd rescued lived there in a high-rise flat. The rooms were small and dark, but they were safe. We were all so happy to see each other again, this time on dry land. In the afternoon, we cooked chicken and rice with a few vegetables, before Doro and I left for his flat again to continue the interview. As we got to the car park to leave, they were taking photos of each other by the car. I knew that later I would see these photos on social media, painting a picture for those back home that their lives in France weren't quite as difficult as they were. And this seems to me to be one of the ways that Europe can be sold as a dream. Social media accounts don't ever reflect reality for any of us, but I knew that back in their home countries, their friends would see a world that didn't exist. Maybe that would form some part of a pull factor. I thought deeply of how much they'd lost for this new life and the awful things that they had faced on their way. Some of them had told me about what had happened to them to make them want to leave in the first place, and along the way, particularly in Libya, I knew that all of them had suffered. The complexity of how I felt about their individual journeys was completely irrelevant by now. None of it matters. They are just people like me and you, and mine and your families, who are battling to build a new future.

We got back to his flat and Doro brought orange juice to the table. I'd been reviewing his first interview, and I asked him if he was ready to continue. There were going to be some tough moments that evening, and I knew it.

'Tell me about Ibrahim. I know he was important to you.'

Ibrahim was a slim guy. So kind. I am looking. I am seeing it. It is like we are sitting together. Ibrahim is a nice guy. Always he used to tell me that to be a man, you must reach for your destiny. That any suffering that you experience will one day finish. That was his belief. And for him, that is where you want to go.

The first day that I met him was in the chat place. The chat place is a working place, where all the workers go. Like all the blacks, they will gather in one place. If anybody needs to carry workers,* they will come to that place. In the morning, they will all get up. There is one big street. Like in Paris. The street, everybody will be sitting. When people come who need workers, he will stand for him, and they will carry the workers. That place, we call it 'chat place', in Tamanrasset.

So, we were sitting together. We did not know each other. After one man came and said that he needed people

* When Doro speaks of 'carrying' people, it usually means taking them from one place to another, or if he talks of carrying workers, he means contracting people to work.

to come and carry cement into his car. As he saw me, he called me and Ibrahim. We go together to drop the cement into his car. After dropping twenty-five bags, the man paid us ten dinars. I took five and Ibrahim took five. It is the first time that I had entered Algeria, and I asked him where we are going to buy food to eat. Ibrahim had been in Tamanrasset already some time. You can buy food for two or three dinar. Ibrahim directed me to a restaurant, and we went to it together. Inside the five dinar, I bought food for us both. We sat down together and ate. It is from there that we know each other. Ibrahim became my best friend in my life.

He told me that he was from Senegal, and I said that I was from Gambia. And we all came together. He said that we all come together because his wife is from Gambia. I said, 'Yes, Senegal and Gambia, they are all the same. We speak all the same languages. We are like family.' It is from there he invited me home. From his five dinar, he also bought things and we went to his home and we cooked Senegalese food. He cooked. As we were eating, he told me to sleep there. I said, 'No, it's OK. I have a place in a camp, so I should go there.' He said, no, let me leave camp and stay with him there. Because in Algeria he was paying rent, so now he lodged me in his house. The following day, we went and collected everything that I had from the camp and went to stay in his house. And we worked together there for more than one year. Every month we paid for the house between us.

Before him I lived in a tent in a camp. Plenty of people lived there. We were sharing everything. Food, work, rent, everything. And it is from there that I heard him say that I can do plenty work. He himself was a painter. He was very fast at painting houses. Very intelligent. He knew his job. He even taught me to paint, and now I can paint how I like it. Every contract that he took, I was the second one who he took to do the job with him. And he was very honest. He was the boss, but when they paid him, he shared the money. He was a friend to me. He was a brother to me. Ibrahim was so kind.

When we used to chat, always he would be smiling. He was never vexed. I never saw him be vexed. But all his life, he needed to do everything quick. He didn't need slow things. Me also, the advice that I used to give him, when we enter some places is to leave things slowly is better, but he needed to do everything fast. He encouraged me to follow this journey, and without him I would have died. When we were in Algeria, I said, 'Let us make money here and then go back to our home country. We can do business between Senegal and Gambia.' I explained about my fishing business: 'We can buy a boat, a new boat, let us work in Algeria, here, maybe two or three years, we will get a lot of money.' He said, 'No, let's go to Europe.' He gave me hope to go to Europe.

After months of writing, I decided to call Doro to go back over this point. What did he mean that Ibrahim gave him hope to go to Europe? In what way was he encouraged to follow this path instead of another? I sent him a text message and arranged a time to call him. Now sat in my own home, with a view through the window into my garden, I set up the recorder and called him. He was ready, and what he told me is something that is covered in this story, but he explains it in a way that I cannot. The authenticity of his voice is crucial because it reflects absolute reality. Softly spoken now, with a gentleness in his voice as he greets me, contrasted by agitated fast talking, as he tries to articulate what is, for him, one of the greatest reasons for people starting this journey and a huge source of frustration for him.

What did you mean that Ibrahim gave you hope to go to Europe?

He used to show me pictures of him friends and him brothers who are in Europe. They are looking good. So all those things are pushing us. They are driving better cars, have better houses but we, we don't know how they will make that. We are thinking that when you enter Europe you have everything. That's the point. It's all about that. The pictures used to fake people. The way you see the pictures and when you come to Europe, you meet the guys and it's not the same. You understand? I mean the guys suffer and they don't have anything. The man is standing with somebody's car and taking picture, with maybe somebody's house, you understand? So that make us false to push to come in Europe.

I can tell you it's not only me. It's affecting the same in the internet. They are putting on good clothes, eating better food and sending them pictures, because it's all about vanity. But I come here in my own mind. To be truth, even to my enemy I will not encourage him to come on this journey. It is not easy.

How we feel and how you people feel is not the same. We think that everything is here. But to be truth, in fact when you work in your country you can get in Europe easily. Europe will come meet you, you understand?

Ibrahim was showing me everything because he want to make it. I want to work in Algeria to have something

and to go back, but he said Europe is easy to have whatever you want. He said everybody is going to Europe.

If I knew I would have all these experiences, I will not
leave Algeria, I will go back. But mankind cannot know.
You will just force yourself. If you never go, you will not
know what is in front, and people, they will all they say to
you is that you should go. They are a liar. They don't know
nothing in front. They just follow the internet and follow
people that say Europe is like this and Libya is no problem, but after you go and enter in the journey, you will see
the problem. In your country, nobody will contact you
and say bring money, bring this amount, and treating you,
and killing people in front of you – even killing you.

It was not just Ibrahim. It was everybody. In that subject, Brendan, there are negatives and positives. In that
time, you have contact in Europe who used to tell you that
Europe is not good, that if you don't have papers, you will
not work. And if you don't work you will not have good
life. You will not have food. You will not have money.
Europe is hard. But some people who are in Europe, they
used to encourage people. Understand?

When we was in Algeria, Ibrahim carry me to one big
house. I can say there was more than 200 immigrants. More
than that. It was a big house. Women, men. Everybody is
there for to go to Europe. And when you stay there for long
time, even if you don't want to go to Europe, you will have
a feeling to come in Europe, because everyone is standing
there to go to Europe. So you feel you will deserve to go to
Europe. You will have that concept to go to Europe because
of them pushing you to go in Europe.

And plenty people, they will have friends, they will show
you pictures of their friends. They are living in Europe. The

video, the post of them living in Europe and they are living in good position. So, you will have a feeling to go Europe. That thing push plenty people to go Europe. For we in Africa, we think when you go to Europe, you have everything. Even if you suffer in Europe, you have everything. But them that are living here, them they know. Them, they don't have nothing. So that is the point. That's why plenty people are in Africa on this journey. The problem is that when they want to come it is because they are seeing something who push them or give them the feeling to come in Europe. It is material or money thing. Or a good life, or a cure. Better health. So all those things make plenty people move to Europe.

There is no single answer as to why people travel into Libya and find themselves on boats crossing the Mediterranean Sea. The perspective that Doro offers is just one aspect of a broader nuance surrounding migratory motivations. People fleeing wars in countries such as Syria, Afghanistan or South Sudan may have completely different ideas as to why people embark on these dangerous crossings. For each person it is different and I certainly respect Doro's perspective here. It is a view that I share, while recognising that this is just one aspect of a much more complicated issue.

Chapter 8

Desert From Algeria to Libya

We decided to enter Libya. The first time that we came to Libya, we paid from where we are in Tamanrasset, from there we go to Ilamane, from there we go Illizi, from there we go to Debdeb;* from Debdeb we took the desert. We paid, but all my money, it was in Ibrahim's hands, because I did not know the journey or how to pack the money, but he was very intelligent. He bought a pot of cream, a big bottle of cream. He put the money into a plastic bag and then he put the bag inside the big bottle of cream. He packed all of our money there and covered it in the cream. They can search all of our bag, like they did in every checkpoint that we came to. The police would search us, and search everything. When they go into the bag they would find the bottle and look inside and see the cream and leave it. They would search our body. They would not see anything. Ibrahim was very intelligent.

We go up to the desert and come down. As we come

* A journey of more than 1,300 km.

down, they told us that the journey is not far, but they cannot carry us to Zintan, because they would be arrested by the police officers. But if we start walking now, by the evening, we will be in the city no problem. As we were coming to the desert, they gave everybody one bottle of water. Everyone was profited to drink the water because it was hot. We were in three small cars, like a jeep. And every jeep was taking eleven, twelve people from Algeria to Libya. They drive us until 12 a.m. and drop us and show us the sign. They gave everybody one bottle of water. The bottle is too small. Some of them profited and they drink all of the water. But me, I was doing small, small because I had already passed another desert. I knew to leave the water. As we march up to the border of Libya, some of them didn't make it. And some of them, we left them behind. I didn't hear about them. I don't know whether they are in the life. I don't know if the animals ate them. I don't know if they died in the desert. I don't know whether they reached where they wanted to go.

As I came directly through that desert, my only thoughts are to go back. But there is no going back. Where you have come from is too far, you would never make it. And you don't know how far you must go. You don't know if you are halfway, nearly there or if you must go back. In the desert you cannot go back, you are just going. You have no compass or nothing. You don't know where you are heading. They just showed you to take this direction and it will take you to the city. And you don't know all the time which direction you are going. Some of them they don't even see the direction, they just walk in the desert until they die, without knowing where they are going. Some follow others. Some of them go group by group. After a while some of them, they would say, 'My friend, it is not this way, you are walking people the wrong way. It is tiring', and we all split into small groups.

It was not like the desert of Mali or Niger to Algeria. This desert is not a long desert, but it is a dangerous desert. The desert is always hot. As we were walking, the sun was hot. Everyone profited the water when they got it, but Ibrahim was very intelligent. He used to drink small, small. Like a soldier. But it was too small for me. I can tell you a lot of things about water. Some people were pissing in their bottles and drinking it later in the day. I saw it with my own eyes. I saw a woman pissing and drinking with a man. I saw the man pissing and giving it to his younger brother to drink. I saw it two times. In the desert, everything that you couldn't imagine is happening there about water. Like some people, they will see the place where the camels drink, a small and dirty water hole in the desert and they drink it. Me too. I found where the camels drink and I drank from the water.

People went mad with thirst and didn't believe each other. Everybody was hungry and thirsty. So nobody was talking. If you were talking, it was a problem. It is from there Ibrahim said to me, 'Boy, come follow me', and we left the group. When Ibrahim told me to leave the small group, I knew I now had to follow Ibrahim. After we were walking throughout the day, no nothing, no houses, no water, and everything was finished. I stopped and took off my bag and took out a biscuit. I started to eat the biscuit, and the biscuit caught me. I was panicking. I didn't have any water. I didn't know what to do. I was choking. I thought I will die. I was so frightened. After, he just came up to me with his bag and took out his own bottle of water and said, 'Boy, I only have small water, but there is no more water for either of us. But you take and drink, to save your life.' I drank the water. He saved my life. I will not forget it. If he didn't give me water, I would have died there.

We started the journey again that night. The city, we saw it in the midnight. We saw lights. We felt so happy, and suddenly we felt safe again. We celebrated with each other. First, we saw cars, before we entered into the city. One car stopped and asked us where we were heading. We asked him, 'Is this Zintan? The city?' And we begged him for water. He gave us water. We asked him to take us to the city, but he said no. When we saw the lights, they were very far away. In the desert, you can see the light from a long way away. We reached in the city in the morning, around 8 a.m. We sit down in the taxi garage. We asked in the garage, and the shopkeeper explained to us every-thing where black people are staying in the city. We must take the taxi and go up to the black people place. He got us a taxi to take there, and it was very expensive. Ibrahim knew the dinars and paid everything. Me, I didn't even ask him. I didn't need to. I just trusted Ibrahim with my money.

The other people, I didn't know about them no more. Some people died in the desert. Me and Ibrahim, we made ourselves to the city, but plenty of people died on the way. In the days after, I saw some people from the group that we left with. They were explaining to me what happened. Out of thirty-six people who started in Algeria, only fifteen or sixteen people made it to the city. The rest died in the des-ert. Some people drank their water quickly because how the people explained the journey. They said that when you walk a small way, you will see the city. So when the sun was hot, people used to drink their drink. Some of them drank all of their water in the day and it was finished. But Ibrahim was very intelligent. It was like he knew the journey. When the people gave everyone their water, I think that he took extra for his bag. He was drinking small water.

When Doro explained how the smugglers lie, it reminded me of what many of the people that we rescue say. In the same way that the smugglers told Doro and his fellow travellers that their journey would be short, often people tell us that the smugglers in Libya tell them that crossing the Mediterranean Sea is just a few short hours. 'It's like a big river.' At night, the fires from the oil fields can be seen from dozens of miles away. Some people have told me that the smugglers have told them that it's a light from Europe, or that you go past these lights, then after only a short while they will be in Europe. We often used to find them less than forty miles from the Libyan coast, which still takes some time on their low-powered engines, although things have changed since then. Such is the way with dynamic political situations and demands of governments. Often the people that we find have been travelling for hours and hours in the sea, sometimes leaving at midnight, only to be found at around lunchtime. Sometimes they spend days at sea, without going far at all. Their flimsy rubber dinghies are not designed to make such dangerous crossings with so many people on board, but the smugglers tell them that they will make it in just a couple of hours. The occasional boat does make it to Malta or Lampedusa, but that's not usually the case. Many will have only made it a fraction of the journey before they are found, or the boat hits the bigger waves, and then breaks up and sinks. They are always amazed when we show them on a map how close they still are to Libya, and that even after many hours at sea, they're around a tenth of the way to where they're heading. Of course, sometimes, boats make it all the way, and some boats are less crowded than others. It's a real lottery though, and the death toll is massive. The smuggler will always benefit from encouraging people to make these crossings, be they at sea, or like here in the desert. They reassure people to make dangerous journeys by telling them lies, all for a little bit of money.

Chapter 9

Arriving in Libya

As we reached in Zintan, in the town, they caught us, and there we lost hope. Because when they caught us, they took our bags. And the cream was in the bag. And the money was inside the cream. But they did not catch us like policemen. They caught us like mafia. They collected everything that we had because we were new. It is those taxi drivers who do that to us. The taxi driver will take us to a place of the mafia. They will take your everything. And the taxi driver will play like he is innocent. And he will say that Libya is like that. They are very wicked. And who else is dealing with them? After they are dealing with the mafia and taking you to the black people place. As he is driving you in the taxi, he will call them, and you don't know their language. And he will explain to them, and they will drop you there. And after they will come and search you and take your money and everything and put you in the prison. But it is not a real prison. It is an abandoned house. So, as they put us there, they took everything. It is like they didn't even close the door. They want us to go. So, in the night, nobody came. Nobody brought us food or drink. And we looked at the window. We pushed the window open, and me and Ibrahim climbed out. After we made our way to Tripoli.

We worked in Tripoli for eighteen months. We stayed in Medina* as builders. In Medina in 2016, it was calm. In Medina, me and Ibrahim were staying in the same place, but we were not working in the same place as each other. Ibrahim was doing painting and I was doing construction. But at the end of every day, we are coming down and we go to the market to buy everything together to cook. We come home and we cook together always because we were in the same house. We were paying rent between us.

One day we were sitting together in the evening. Ibrahim was telling me about the time he went to Gambia. When he first entered into Gambia, he didn't know the address of his family. It was his first time to leave Senegal. As he got there, he lost the address. He said that one day he was sleeping in the streets. He didn't know that in Gambia there would be thieves. He left his bag and shoes under his head and slept in the streets until the morning, waiting to find his parents. As he got up in the morning, he didn't see his bag. He didn't see his shoes or anything. He said Gambian people are very smart thieves. Always he teased me of this. Every time he used to laugh with me about the people of Gambia, because Gambia is small, and he is from Senegal. Ibrahim is a kind guy and a funny guy. He always made me laugh.

When we were in Tripoli, we decided to gather together to be one, to work together. We were best friends because

* An area within Tripoli.

we did not die in the desert. We survived. In Libya my first job was working in construction as a labourer for the builders, giving them blocks, cement, and water and everything that they needed. It was a hard job to survive and earn money to cross the Mediterranean. After one year six months in Libya, we had earned enough money to pay. We paid the smuggler for the trip. Everybody paid 1,000 [dinar].

Chapter 10

Crossing the Sea

After the first couple of days of interviewing Doro, I'd drawn up an order of events. It was important to go back and get detail, but it was even more important to manage the recounting of such events. This was a traumatic retelling of what had happened, and it seemed to me that Doro had blanked much of it out. I could see how his eyes changed focus as he put himself back in that time, the first time, sat on the comfortable chairs in front of his television. A black and white movie played in the background, turned down almost to mute. French-speaking characters flickered through some medieval film as the glow of the screen lit up his face in the darkness.

Doro needed a break at times and that required a patient approach. Sometimes we were interrupted by the distraction of the film or a cigarette break. I could see how this was affecting him, but I could also see courage and determination to get the job done. I could tell when he needed a break and this chapter is the result of going back to this point in time on several occasions, even after I returned to England, when I was able to call Doro to go back over the detail. In the first

interview, in Doro's flat, I asked him how he paid the smugglers, and how he made it to the sea. Later we went back over
it, piece by piece.

I was inside my house. I had come for a walk in the evening after I had come home from work. My landlord he
tells me and said that there is one Arab woman who wants
to push today.*

'Do you want to go to Italy?'

I say, 'Yes.'

'You have money?'

I say, 'Yes. How much?' He says that it is 1,000 dinar,
like 650 euros [at the time]. I say, 'Yes, I get it.' But at that
time in Libya getting that much money is a hard job because
to get money is too hard. So the man explained to me that
I will need to get the money, because there are some people
who will come out in that house. It was a rented house in
Tripoli. All blacks rented this house in Tajura.† I said yes,
no problem. You want me to give you the money, he say
yes, so I paid him.

After we cook, around eight or nine at night, he come
and knock on the door. He called us people, me, Ibrahim
and one boy, a Guinea boy. He come to us and tell us to sit
down by the main door. One car will come and collect us.
I was nervous of being cheated and sold because when I
came and sat down in front of the door with the boy, I was
asking the boy, 'Do you trust this man? Is he selling us? Is
he going to take our money and then sell us thinking he

* When Doro says 'push', he is talking about sending a boat of
people out to sea.
† A small town 23 km east of Tripoli.

will get money?' He said that he trusted the landlord and that he isn't like that. I believed him because he had stayed in that house for a long time. After the car came, he called the landlord, and told us to get into the car.

I said, 'No, I will not enter.' He said that Mohamed tells us to come and collect you from the door here.

I said, 'I want you to call the landlord so I can speak to him.' After he called my landlord, I talked to him on the phone. When we got into the car, there were already another two people in the car. Now we were five in the back. Those two people were from Sudan. We speak to them in French and English and they don't speak it. If we try to speak to them in Arabic, the man who is driving the car will understand. But I was not comfortable because I did not know what would happen next. I had never experienced Libya pushing,* so I was nervous. We rode in the car for about thirty minutes. He left the main road and entered into the bush. As he entered into the bush for the first time, me, I tell Ibrahim like this: 'It's finished, they are going to sell us, we are not going to the beach.' After, we panicked in the car. We don't know what to do. We are five in the back. He friend is in the passenger seat with a gun. So now I asked the driver in Arabic, 'Where are you carrying us?'

He said, 'You don't want to go Europe?'

I said, 'Of course, but this way is not Europe.'

He said, 'You people are going to the seaside. Just calm down. We don't need too much noise. After twelve we push these people.'

From there I started to get small, small calm. After then we went up to the beach side. They took us to the small

* Being smuggled.

room. We entered there and we meet plenty people who are heading to cross the sea. After, they went and fetched more people. When I was sitting there, I saw more than three times they went to fetch more people, but we met some people there. After 12 o'clock we sat down, and everybody was complaining. Some people needed the toilet. Some people needed to drink. Some were hungry. I stay here for a long time, and I don't get a place to sit. Some people are insulting each other. Some people were fighting. Because if you want to move, you will stand on somebody's leg. The place is hard, like a small room. If you put more than seventy people together, they will start insulting each other.

That man that push us, his name is Abdul. He is very very good. He respect his job. But later, when I was in Zuwara,* I heard that they killed him. They shot him by a gun. It was his own crew that were working with him in a place called Grigarage.† But with the money he used to get, he wasn't fair with his crew. That's what they say. I heard that somebody came to meet him in his house and shoot him. Abdul was a good man with us though. He did not treat us badly. Even his people never beat black people in front of him. They had guns, but they never threatened blacks in front of Abdul. The only day he made blacks suffer is the day he want to push. He will carry everybody and put you in a single room.

At around 12, they come. We hear them coming. Everybody is small. Nobody talking. You see, in Libya, Arab

---

* A coastal town, around 100 km west of Tripoli and departure point for refugee boats.
† One of the most dangerous neighbourhoods in Tripoli, with strong links to the slave trade.

people are like God. When you hear them, you will not talk until they pass. Because they can do anything to you. There is no law. There are no police. If you go to the police and tell them that a man stole from you, they will ask you where your papers are. If you bring your paper, they will ask you why you come to our country. You want to cross. That's why you come to our country. They will go and lock you. After locking you up they will sell you. The police officers themselves. There is no law. Every immigrant knows that. There is no law. Anything that you do to me is OK.

They get some people who know how to make the boat. They take three or four people. You people will come make all the boat that night. And they will put the air inside the boat and the boat will be heavy. When the time comes to push, everybody will come out and say *la 'illah 'iilaa allah** and carry the boat. So you go round the boat and carry the boat on our shoulders. We marched for twenty or thirty minutes with the boat on our shoulders until we reached the water. We were all so tired. Some people they want to leave the boat and the boat is hard for the other people. The smuggler shoots his gun up into the sky and shouts, 'Everybody will carry the boat!' because he knows that if we drop the boat, the boat will spoil. It is so heavy because the engine is on the boat, the petrol and everything. Everybody was tired.

When we dropped it into the water, everybody come back to the room again. They left three or four people to stay with the boat and keep it balanced in the water. They will enter inside the water and catch the boat. Everybody

* There is no god but Allah.

else goes back to the room. The smuggler waits by the door. He called us out one by one, and we followed. Two people escorted us to the water, and we jump onto the boat one by one until just the people holding the boat are left. Then the captain will enter and then the people.

When Doro talks of a captain, he's referring to the driver of the rubber boat that they're travelling in. Most of the people that cross the Mediterranean will be at sea for the first time in their lives. They have simply no idea what to expect and will be very scared. Few of them have any experience of the sea, and the smugglers don't want to risk taking them to Europe them-selves, so they offer a reduced rate for anyone who is prepared to take the controls. The European authorities take a dim view on those who 'captain' the boats, but often, it's just some guy who has no money and tells the smuggler that he can do it. If they're lucky, their 'captain' will have driven a boat at some point in the past or will naturally take well to the controls. Often, we as rescuers find people on the boats who don't know how to turn the engines off. Usually though, after a few hours at sea, they will have figured it out. The same goes for the 'compass man', a reduced rate for the man prepared to hold a satellite phone, or a handheld compass, that often doesn't even point north.

The first time I came in Libya we was in Tajura, you understand, they push us. From Tripoli, they push us. That man who push us is a very good man. He name is Abdul. He didn't have any problem. But the only problem is that he didn't look up the weather. The time he was pushing us the water was good, but after midnight the water was spoiling. The sea was not good.

After everybody enter the boat, him push the boat up to maybe one or two kilometres inside the water. After him enter the speedboat, give the boat to the captain to carry us. The clouds were black and blue, and after some time, we start to see some stars. And the air is plenty windy. We enter into the water, we go up to the middle of the sea. There is plenty problem. People they are talking because that time the water is not good. You understand? It was the weather. The people are saying that there is plenty air and water was coming inside, so the boat, it started to move to the left and right because of the waves.

When the water started to spoil, inside the boat, people started to query. People started to talk. Understand? Now nobody had a good heart. Everybody had a bad heart. Everybody was panicking thinking him will die. Ibrahim was in the front. Me, I was in the place that they put the fuel. But after the weather started to spoil, we come together. Me, I go front. I go and meet him and tell him don't worry. Me, I know the water very well. Nothing will happen to us, I used to advise him at that time.

When the weather started to spoil, the waves in the water knock our boat. Inside the rubber boat, there is wood in the bottom. When the water knocked the boat, the wood in the middle started to crack and spoil. The wooden boards in the bottom of the boat started to split. People in the middle started to go front. Some people started to go back. And people started pushing each other. But me and Ibrahim, where we are, we are still there sitting. When the wood split, in that area we started to have problems with holes in the rubber tubes and the boat started to reduce. The air started to come out of the rubber and the water was coming in the centre of the boat.

And the boat started to come together. It was like if you take a carton of juice, and you fold it in the middle, and the front touch the back.

Since the wood in the middle of the boat cracked, we don't have any hope. The compass man, he have the telephone and I see him call. He called the Libyan peoples. The man he spoke to spoke in Arab, and we tell him we are not in international. It is Tripoli people we call. Before the marines come, some people they are fighting. They are pushing each other. Some people push forwards, and some people push back and before we know, the boat have more problem and plenty people are lost in the water.

Some people they are unconscious. Some people they are hurt. Some people are praying to God. Some people were calmed down. But some people are talking with the captain and insulting him. They were pushing each other. It is from there plenty people are lost in the water, not only because of the boat scatter that people lost in the water. It is because plenty people are scared. Plenty people are feared. They was fighting each other. When people come to one side, others, they would push them back and tell them to go that side and before they can go, the boat spoil. All the front of the boat come down of air and into the water.

The people all come to the front, the captain said we all come to the front, and only the fuel and the machine are in the other side, where the water are. Plenty people fell in the water. Plenty people. Some people say that they know how to swim, and we are not far because we are still in Libyan water. So they went to swim, but all those people, they died. Because that time nobody can swim in that water. The water is bad, and the weather is not good.

You cannot swim up to 50 km when the weather is that bad.

The people left in the boat is less than seventy people and the man pushed one hundred-and-something people from Tripoli. Maybe fifty people, they died. They just lost. Men, women, and young men. Nigerian women, there are plenty. It is them I remember too much. They were praying to Jesus: 'Oh Jesus Christ, oh Jesus Christ, oh Jesus Christ. Help us Jesus. That we not die here. Help us and our family. Oh Jesus Christ.' I remember them praying. And Muslims too! They are praying. 'Help us, help us!' Everybody was praying and you cannot hear no one, and then in a small time, you will see somebody fall inside the water. And the boat, where the boat have problems, where the water enter into the boat, those people that are sitting there, I think plenty people are lost.

After, we started to call. When we call, the people is not Europe. It is Oussama who come. He is Libyan peoples' coastguard. It is they who rescue us, but by that time some people lost. We didn't see them. And the way also Oussama was helping us, he was giving us rubber rings. You will catch the rubber to enter in the big boat, you understand? Them, they surrender our boat with guns. So there also some people that were lost with this. But nobody will mind them.

Before they come, we lost plenty of people. At 4 a.m. our boat have problem. Oussama come at around 7 a.m. We all happy to see him because he come to rescue us. They came first with speedboat, like you guys, but with guns. After they realise that they cannot carry our boat, so they call the big boat. Before the big boat arrived, it took almost one hour. They didn't take any of us on to their speedboat, they only give us some small rubber rings. They put the rubber inside the water. It's like the rubber rings that Sea-Watch have. It's the small rubbers they throw to the people.

Me, I give the rubber ring to other people, because me I know how to float in the water. Me, I didn't get lost, but the first people who rushed to catch the rubber rings in the water, some of them lost. Because the time they throw us the rubber, they tell us to take it easy. To take one and one to come, but people, they are jumping. It was panic. Everybody wanting to come in the boat. After me I say to Ibrahim, don't worry, we will take our time. And people they will do fisher fisher. After, we will go.

Plenty people are panicking. Plenty people are jumping to catch the rubber rings. Some people they will jump and catch the rubber, but they will catch the rope that is tied to the rings and leave the rubber. They will fall down. No Libyan people will help them. Even the lifejacket they didn't give. They didn't give lifejackets to nobody.

In the end they throw us rubber. Small rubber rings from inside the big boat when it arrived. So we will catch and put in our legs and they will throw ropes and we will climb up the ropes on to the big boat and we will go and sit down. But some people they are wounded, so they carry them. A Red Cross man bring us small things inside the boat and put things on our wounds. They said we are not going back to the prison, we will go back to our country, but first we will go to Zuwara prison.

Some people they are wounded because the fuel of the water touch their body. Me myself, I was wounded from the fuel and the water. When the fuel and the water mix, you will wound. So plenty of people were wounded. After they carry plenty people to hospital. Me, I didn't need to go to hospital.*

So we meet plenty people on the big boat. They are from Sudan, Mali, Senegal people, plenty people and they said that they were also caught by this boat. So we people, we remain and Oussama carry us to him prison. So we meet plenty of other people from other boats there. He catch plenty boats, more than ten or fifteen boats. I can say, because that time Italian people say they don't need immigrant people. I think that the Italian people are sponsoring Oussama. He is a bad man. Those other people said, before they catch us, they catch two boats. And those people, they said that they scatter their boats. They catch them. They burn their boats, their fuel and everything. They just take the machine. After then, we are the third boat that they catch that very day.

They all saw us in the water and that was on the news. When you check the news in 2016, you will see us. That's our boat. The big boat had a big place at the back of the boat, and the people are all sitting there. Some of them, they say they are pushed from Sabratha. Some of them push from Zuwara. We were pushed from Tripoli. After everybody came to the big boat, they shoot our boat in the place that have air, and the boat sink.

The only thing they tell us is ask why we go to Europe. The way is closed, and the water is not good. And a white man asked us how many people we are before the boat sink. He is a journalist. There was a Red Cross man, I think,

* When petrol mixes with salt water it has a corrosive effect on skin. Such 'fuel burns' are common injuries that we as refugee rescue workers have to deal with.

who speak to me in English in the big boat, but the man in the small boat was a journalist. He come with the Libyan coastguards. He was an Italian man. I was speaking with him in English. He said he was working for the Red Cross. He was on the Libyan coastguard boat. Nobody was hurt in front of him on the ship. After we got back to Libya though, everybody suffered.

On the ship I saw the white man, I was talking with him in English. He said we are not going to prison. He said they will take us home. I said, 'That's good. If you can take me to my home country, that is good. I don't need to go to the prison. Because we just want to cross to Europe.' He started to ask us what we would do in Europe: 'When we go to Europe what will we do there?' He said Europe is not good. Europe didn't get us people nothing. People that get there, they are suffering. After they come down,* they carry us to the prison of Zawia.† We were back in Libya. In Zawia they said that they would deport us, but a black man is a diamond in Libya. A black man is money in Libya.

* 'Take us from the big boat.'
† A notorious detention centre 45 km west of Tripoli, commonly known as Osama Prison after its infamous commander, who has known links to the slave trade, torture and many forms of brutal extortion.

Chapter 11

Bani Walid

In the UK and Europe, and on social media platforms, you will find lots of opinions on what should happen to the people who try to make it to Europe, many believing that we should simply 'send them back'. As if there were no reasons for them leaving their home countries in the first place, and no reason at all not to return them there, or to Libya. In the UK, few even understand that many who brave the English Channel have already survived the Mediterranean. Fewer still have any idea what happens to those who are returned to Libya.

The 1951 Refugee Convention, along with the Geneva Convention, were written to ensure that some of the horrors that happened during and immediately after the end of World War II were never repeated. Millions of people who were forcibly deported from their homelands in mass evacuations and brutal ethnic-cleansing operations attempted to gain international protection, which was often denied, and many were subsequently tortured and killed. The Convention laid down laws and guidelines to ensure the proper treatment of displaced people and to protect their human rights. The added 1967

Protocol expanded the scope of the Convention to cover the rest of the world as displacement by war, famine, political unrest, or natural disaster increased. The cornerstone of the refugee convention is Article 33, which prohibits the return of refugees to a country where they might face persecution on the grounds of their race, religion, nationality, membership of a particular social group, or on the grounds of their political opinions.

Currently, and for a long time now, European governments have been funding the Libyan Coast Guard, supplying boats and providing training. By funding these groups to capture and return people at sea, often in international waters, we are simply paying the Libyans to do our dirty work for us. We are circumventing the refugee convention, bypassing laws that we wrote in order to protect people and essentially contributing to their suffering by proxy.

In Libya, there are detention centres where those that are captured at sea are taken. One of the most well-known of these camps is Zawia, 45 km west of Tripoli. It was and still is notorious for its inhumane conditions, suffering and abuse. The IOM (International Organisation for Migration) ran a 'voluntary humanitarian return programme' from the detention centres, where people were given the choice between a 'voluntary' return to their home country or indefinite abusive detention.

They take me and my friend Ibrahim. We were together in Zawia. Because in Zawia they had people from many boats. It is not just our boat. I was in Zawia for two weeks. They tell you that Red Cross and MSF [Médecins Sans Frontières] will come and check you people and give you broth, soup, clothes for deporting. And from Zawia, they should carry you people and take you to Tripoli. What they tell us is simple: that they take us from here and we will leave the Arab world. They said they will deport us to our own country because Oussama catch sixteen boats and there plenty people in the camp.

We were so happy to enter into the bus. There were eleven or twelve buses, but only six buses reach the airport. The other buses were sold. As we entered into the bus, some buses reached into the airport. The other six buses take another route. I was on the other bus. They take us to Bani Walid. Direct to the prison. And everybody will come out money. To sell us makes the Libyans more than the money that the Libyans take to deport people. It's such bad luck. My bus was such bad luck.

In the prison of Bani Walid, it is a real prison. There is no escaping. It is like Guantanamo in America. Because is facing a sea of desert. It is a small city. Before, in history, in the time of the president, when they catch the criminals, it is there that they carry them go. So, in Bani Walid, I entered into the prison and when I got there, I really know that I am in a prison. It's really shit. As we reached the prison, they now carry everybody, one by one to single rooms. When we enter into the room they will come and search you, from top to bottom. They will search your everywhere. They even search some people inside their anus because they say that they put the money there. Anything that you have got for your body, they will control it. That's why nobody cannot get a look to take a picture.

They searched me, but I never took off my clothes. Because as I come before they searched me, I took everything out of my pockets and gave it to them. I put it on the table. And I told them, 'I give you my everything, there is nothing else, only that.' So, the man searched me and believed me because I was wearing loose clothes. Not plenty pockets. From the search, they carry you and you go and sit down in the sun before you enter in the cells. When you sit down in the sun, for some hours they will finish searching everybody. They will carry everyone to the prison, and you will not see the sun again until the day comes that they come to treat you.

In Ben Walid I don't know the price they sell me for, but it is not much money. You cannot know the price they sell you for because you will not be present. Like you are in the prison. The Arab people, they will deal with each other. They will come to see each other and deal to their house. In the following day they will go get the car and go collect everybody that they sell in that place.

First, they put me in a big cell, more than 600 metres, like a warehouse, and everybody get their own sponge [mattress]. Some people, they are sick. They died there in front of us. They take them and beat them, bring them back and they die in front of us. In the morning you will take their place. Somebody is sick or died, if you come new, you will take their place without changing nothing. They will not change the sponge. They will not change the cover. They will not change nothing. You are not taking bath. Because where people used to drink, if you go and say you will take a bath there, they will get problem with people in the cells, because it is the only water we get to drink. The toilet water. The food is 7 o'clock. At 7 o'clock they come and give you one bottle of water and half bread. Until 7 again and they give you one bread and one water.

For the first time in that prison, I see the food is the first sufferance. It is the first wickedness. In the morning at

7 a.m. they give you one bread for two people and one bottle of water, up to 7 p.m. again. And you will eat it by force. If you run out of water, you must go to the pipe of the toilet and take water to drink. If somebody go to the toilet, it is the same water they drink. I ask: what the hell is that? They tell me: money or die. No pity. No pity for no one. And no protection. And only sufferance.

The second thing I imagined I see in that prison when they was to treat you, they will take off all your clothes. Like your mother born you. And they will tie you up by your hands. And they will tie your legs down. You cannot do nothing. And they will use you with telephone and they tell you to make a video call. And they will maltreat you. Beating you. Wounding you with knife. Torture you for your parents to see you suffering, so they will bring you money. And when they bring you to that prison, so you must pay the money.

They sell us because the black man is a business in Libya. It's not only me. Every black man in Libya is money. It is not only me they are selling. They sell lots of people. Before I was in Libya, they were selling people, and still now that I have come out from Libya, they are selling people. That's their business. How they make money. They sell you so that the buyer can torture you to take money from your family. They demand that your parents give them money. That money is bigger than everything. My mother, my father and family, nobody can get this money. And even my father, who is dead, cannot have this money in all his life.

And some people, they will go. There are six or seven people and they have guns. There is nothing you can do. Not anything you want to do. They can shoot you and you will die. You will suffer until the morning comes. You will suffer until you die. And they are laughing. Beating you with laugh. Torture you with laugh. And nobody will tell you they are sorry. And you will die if you don't do nothing. They are forcing you to bring the money. The amount, you cannot get it. If for me, the amount they ask, if I get it, I will not have come out of my country, I would have stayed in my country and do business, because it is my country.

We don't do nothing. They just see us, we want to cross the Mediterranean in our boats. And go to Europe and leave their country. They are so evil. I see them in their eye, and I see them in their movement. And how they torture somebody, I know they are somebody who is like an animal. Everybody living in Libya knows Bani Walid.

When I was in the prison, when I was first there, I don't know the situation. I was asking everybody in the cells. Until the third day, I see they bring someone. He was crying. All his body was wounded. I came closer to him and asked him what happened. He cannot stand or explain me nothing. At four in the morning he also died, my brother.

Doro's face contorted with the memory of what he had seen. I wanted to stop the interview. I let him talk. He wanted to release it, but I could see, hear and feel how much this hurt. At times he spoke so quickly, with a burst of energy. At times he released his story slowly and softly. Here, he paused, composing himself until he was ready to start again.

Plenty people died in front of me. I know them in the life. I know them in the prison. They are all good and gentle guys. I cannot count how many of them died. And there were plenty of cells. I could not see everything that was happening. Some cells, you will hear them say that somebody died. Some cells, you will not see. And nobody in the cell will explain you nothing because there are plenty people that when they go outside, they will not come back. Some, when they come back their wounds are OK, but they die. They cannot explain what happened inside that treating place until the day that you yourself will be there and see what they will do to you.

Bani Walid was controlled by Matammud. And another man who controlled Ben Walid, he was one guy. There is another man, Ya Ali, who is an Arab man, he is a military chief that they give the money we pay. And another man. A black man like me. He is from Gambia. His name is Sankung. He was getting his own gun and his own crew. And the crew that he had was only the big people from Cameroon and Nigeria. Those other African countries, the tough guys. There are about six people. It is them who will catch you and tie you. After, you will come and after they deal with the other man. The other man also get his own gun. His nickname is Tupac, but his real name is Matammud, it is a Muslim name. He is the one who sell you. He is from Grigarage in Tripoli.

It is not uncommon for rescue workers to hear stories of torture, to see the scars, and to hear of the most incredible cruelty. So many people on the ship explain how they were beaten, starved, sold and raped. The stories emerging from Libya speak consistently of systemic abuse. Doro's story in this respect is not unusual at all. Reliving this torture was in itself torture for Doro, as it is for every person who is seeking asylum.

Doro

When the smuggling trade started to diminish, the militias changed their methods of making money. Ransom calls are made to parents who sell everything they own to help their children survive. Many of them can't pay the demands, so they create Facebook appeals to save their children, bringing in money from all of their community. Those whose families pay for them to be released then face the guilt of returning home empty-handed, knowing that their families have given everything for their release. For some, it drives them to try again in desperation to reach Europe and eventually repay and make good what their parents have paid. It's such an incredibly sad situation.

Chapter 12

The Death of a Lion

When we were in the prison, everything changed with Ibrahim. It's like the man has seen that he will never come out. It was like he died. He didn't used to sleep at night. He used to chat until the morning. Sometimes I would explain to him that I am trying to sleep. He would talk, and say, 'Boy, no, we will die. This time I know it is finished. I know Bani Walid. It is finished.'

The way he was talking was angry and anxious. He would not talk small, like the Ibrahim I know. That time, it was always serious talk. No sleeping. When I wake in the morning, I asked him, 'What happened?' I said, 'Boy, we will come out of here, don't worry. One day you will explain to people what happened.'

He said, 'Boy, you don't know nothing! The first day we came here and we saw somebody, and they died in the morning. You don't see that?'

I said, 'Yes, of course I see that, but it will not happen to us. We will do everything to escape here.'

I tried to give him hope and told him to believe in his

heart. He said, 'Here you cannot use your heart, because the prison is surrounded by guards, and everywhere there are guns. And they are treating people every day. Coming and taking people every day and breaking them. Some people, you will hear that people pay but we have no money.'

His parents are alive, but Ibrahim told me that when he called his parents to tell them that he is coming to Libya to cross, his mother was the first person who told him, 'Don't go, don't follow this journey, come back to the house.' He said that he needed to go to Europe. That's why he disobeyed his own mother. In that time, he didn't have any hope to call his parents to explain to them that he is in prison. And he didn't get any mind how to escape. He didn't sleep in the night.

After the fourth day they came for him. He was gone for a long time. After they treated him, they bring him back and he was not crying, but he was bleeding. He was bleeding so much. From his back and everything. I took his t-shirt and demanded water from the friends in another cell. I put the water and started to clean him. He said to me, 'Boy, don't disturb yourself. Me I am already cut.'

They beat him so much that everything was cut. Up inside of him everything was cut. Even his heart, in his chest and his back. His heart was not beating correctly. He saw himself dying and told me not to forget to call his parents. After, I started to cry. I remember that he took his hand and put it on my knee. He said, 'Don't cry.' It was the last time he touched anything. He said, 'Don't cry, you will make it.' His last words he tells me are 'Boy, I think you are getting the address of my mom and my wife?' I said yes. He said, 'Don't forget this address. I believe and trust you. You will come out of this place. But me, I don't think so.'

I was so crying and everyone in the cells was following me and crying. Everybody was sitting and crying. But they were not crying for Ibrahim. They were crying for themselves. Me, I was crying for my best friend. But they are crying, for they know that this thing will happen to them one day.

I said, 'Ibrahim relax.' I take our blanket and put it on top of him. In the night, I got up to him. I said, '7 o'clock, take your bread.' He was responding only in grunts. I said, 'Boy, it's OK.' And then we slept together. In the morning, I woke up. Ibrahim never woke up. Yeah brother, Ibrahim never woke up my friend.

My friend, he was a lion in the desert. But he was not a lion in the prison.

As he said those few words, Doro broke completely. Tears streamed down his face. He stood, with tears flowing onto his t-shirt and left for his bedroom. I fetched him a cigarette. I told him it was OK. I knew it was not. I opened a bottle of beer, and together, we raised a glass to his best friend. Sold and killed for no reason at all. He should be home with his family. Instead, he faced an unimaginable torture, and breathed his last breath in Doro's arms.

Doro was determined to continue the story; his turn in the treatment room was yet to come. I changed the conversation first, talking of happier times, as I didn't know how much more my friend could take. Reliving this cruelty was a torment that I struggle to comprehend. His determination to tell his story, despite the pain that it gave him, shows his strength and his understanding, because he believes that when enough people have been told what is happening, something will change for those that were left behind, and for those that replaced him on this conveyor belt of human suffering. I am not so confident of ever seeing such a change in humanity.

The next day, over breakfast, it was the last day that I would be able to interview Doro. I had to leave first thing the following morning. I was sipping my orange juice, contemplating what had been said the day before, barely knowing how to approach asking Doro if he wanted to continue. He looked up at me. 'Are you ready? I want to tell you about the treatment.'

Chapter 13

Unlucky for Some

Three days later, it was my turn. In the morning when I get up, they bring bread. We eat. I see two guys come to the door. Arab men with guns, and their faces are so wicked. If you see them, you will really know they are killers. One of them got the clothes of a soldier. And the other is dressed in Arab clothes and they call out my name. I come and stand by the door. As I come outside, I see that man Sankung, with his crew. There are about six people.

They escorted me to the treating rooms. As we entered into the treating rooms, they turned off all the lights. As they turned off the lights, they passed me a phone and said, 'Now call your parents.' I explained to them that my father was dead, and that my mother didn't get anything to survive. 'If you torture me and beat me every day and every night, the money will not come. It is better to kill me once. It is more important than to torture me. And you will never get any money from me.'

I said that I don't have any numbers. After they turned on the lights again, they tied me, with my hands up to the iron on the roof. They will tie you on your handcuffs and up. It's like a handcuff, but not like a European handcuff. It is like a dog's rope, like an iron dog's leash. They will tie your hands. And they will tie your feet with rope. And then they hang me from one beam crossing the ceiling, like a chicken place. A pipe. They will tie you up there. They will take off all your clothes. You are naked. And they tied my legs and my feet.

I was thinking that this would be a beating and after, they will let me go. I was thinking I can get luck. After beating me maybe I will live. My heart was beating, I cannot even talk. After, I said to the man, 'What are you going to do to me?'

He said, 'When I have finished with you, their money must come. Even if your father is dead. Money must come. Even if your mom and everything dies, the money must come.'

The man who tied me is not the man who beat me. He go out and three people come back. One came with a gun and started shooting around me. 'If you will not call, we will kill you,' he shouted. 'Take the telephone, calla mama.' Shoot shoot. 'Calla familia!' They displayed the gun, but still I didn't make the call. Afterwards they started the treating. Afterwards I did call my mom, but not that time. I was bleeding so much. 'Calla mama, calla familia,' and it went on like this all the time. And I was shouting as they were beating. In that room you can shout any loud and nobody will hear you screaming outside. It is a detention room; they all really organise it.

So I was crying, 'If you want to kill me, do it. I don't have anybody for you to call.' They were beating me and beating me, until after I cannot cry. I cry until after I cannot cry. I need water to drink, no water. I fed up now and I stopped even feeling them beating me. When they beat you and beat you until you get wounds, you don't care. You cannot feel the beating. The wounds, you cannot feel it. My friend, you go up to now. They beat me up until I vomit blood. But God save me. I will not die in that prison. They beat my head, stomach, back, shoulders, arms. All this is beating marks [shows me the scars]. They beat me until I vomited blood.

Then, after a time, they bring someone they called Tahilla. He is the most wicked man.* He said to me, 'My friend. Take the phone and call your people before I start with you because if not, even if your father and your mother die, if I start to treat you, you must bring money.' That is the most wicked man in the camp. Everybody know him. When he was entering in the camp, he used to shoot guns. Everywhere. Some people say that one day he entered, he saw a Guinean boy and shot him for no reason. The boy was a cook for the prisoners, and he was just shot for nothing.

I was getting information before my turn. As he carried me to the treating house, Tahilla hang me up and took out his knife. He took out the phone. The first mark he made was on my face. He spoiled my face. He demolished and disformed my face with the first one. The second one he gave in my hand because I don't want to catch the phone.

---

* His real name is Osman Matammud. Matammud has since been arrested in Italy after he was recognised by other asylum seekers in a migrant camp in Italy. He was convicted of murder and multiple counts of torture and was said to have raped many women. He was given a life sentence in Italy in 2017.

It was a Rambo knife. And now he said, 'My friend, just take the phone and call your parents.' And I took the phone and called my mom. And my mom started to see the blood and she cried. All the family started to cry and think that I will die in the prison because of all of the blood that she could see. Then they just released me. I was lying on the ground. As I was lying like this [shows me the foetal position], I tried to defend myself and he cut all my arms and chest. And then he spoke to my mom and told her how she will pay the money.

After, they took me back to the prison. They called Sankung; they are working with him. So my mom should give you people money and he will do the transfer and the money will come to Libya. And they stopped beating me. They took me to the cells. That was the first day. Because I talked to my parents. But the money never came. As it come to the following day, they didn't touch me.

Chapter 14

Treatment – Day Three

The third day they came again they come at me, and the man Osman Mattamud said that my mom never paid them any money. So they should treat me, for them to call again. When he came to treat me he was smiling. He said my mom will pay the money. He was happy to treat me. He was happy to do me wickedness. He looked like a wicked man. He was happy to do anything to me. He was smiling because he thought that he will get the money. He enjoyed it. He was so happy.

It is there that I now explained to the man: 'Are you not a Muslim?' Because they tied me, they wanted to beat me. 'What did I do? I didn't steal. I didn't do nothing. I paid my money to cross, and they bring me here. You are treating me like a slave. Like you are not from God. Like you will not die! It is better that you kill me, and when you kill me you must join me, because you will not leave alive. You must die. Everybody will die.' And I said what God say in the Quran. He said, 'When you see your fellow Muslim, just help him. Don't do bad things and then say

"Allah, Allah".' I told him that I will see him in Jannah, and I will not forget.

The thing made him so vexed. He come out at me and pulled out the knife from his jacket. He took it from the scabbard and said, 'You say I don't believe in God?' I said to him, 'When you believe in God, you will not treat someone like an animal. Even animals, nobody will mistreat them. When you want to kill him, you will kill him to eat him.' He went so angry. And then he came with his army knife.

'Look at me,' he shouted. He didn't know what to do. He just stabbed me in the stomach and then I fell down. I was bleeding. As he stabbed me, I took my stomach, and bent over, and then fell onto my knees and then I fell down. I was bleeding. I was bleeding. I stayed there for two hours. It is there that I lost comprehension. When he stabbed me, it was very fast. He is not the man who is used to killing people, but the words I told him made him pay. He decided to eliminate me.

That very day, my mom had paid them. That day it was due for the money to enter the bank and that day nobody should have treated me. They should just come to me and give me the phone and my mom confirm that the money entered. But they did not know. They treated me instead.

Doro hadn't spoken to his mother since before their departure from the Libyan coast. She knew nothing of his capture and return. The first thing that she knew of his return to Libya was when his captors called her on video call; her son tied up, covered in blood and crying for help, with men beating his body and cutting his face as she watched. I have my own children, and I can't imagine how she must have felt seeing and hearing that happen.

Doro found out later that she had paid them as agreed, but that the money must have taken some time to show up in their bank account. In fact, she did as every mother would have done, and did all she could to save her son. The family home that Doro grew up in was sold for a fraction of its value, as she scraped together every single penny that she could find. The need to sell the house quickly meant that she had to accept whatever money she was given. She took the money, rented just a small part of the house back from the person that she sold it to, and sent the money to her son's torturers just as soon as she was able to get it, but it was too late. Doro had already been stabbed and his body taken away.

Chapter 15

The Crocodile Hole

I come unconscious and I don't know what happened after.
I just wake up and see myself in the hole. In the hole, there
were plenty of dead bodies. It was a grave where they threw
me. I think that when I went unconscious, they just carried
me in a car to where they throw all the dead bodies. There
were many dead bodies in there. I still think about this
when I talk to my psychologist in France. Every time when
I sleep, even in the sea, every time that I was sleeping, I used
to dream of that hole. It is like when I was in the hole.

It was unimaginable. I have never seen anything like
this in my life. Nobody has seen anything like this, except
for the Arab people who were working in that prison.
When I explain Libya to my friends, they know the hole.
Everybody knows about the hole because they hear about
the hole. They call it Bambadinka.*

* In researching for this book, I was told that Bambadinka means
'the crocodile hole', also the name given to an infamous cell in the
Gambian National Intelligence Agency HQ.

The hole is like a tractor dug the hole. And the hole is like a balancing hole. It goes up and down. Like a tractor digging. So how I think it happened, because I saw the tracks, they come to the big place where they throw you, and you fall down on the bodies. And when it was time to climb out, it was not happy, because you come through how the tractor dug. I had to climb out of all the dead bodies. There were plenty of bodies.

Some of them, they rust. You will see only bones. Some of them are dead since the time of the revolution. I think so. I think the hole was at first more deep than the time they throw me in there. It was deeper before, but now it is filled with dead bodies, until it is full. I wake up. I didn't see anything first. My heart didn't touch anything, because me myself, I didn't know where I was, who I was, and what brought me there. And I didn't know how I should get up.

When I wake up, I was lying on my side, on top of dead bodies. I was on the top. After I see for myself, I got up. My eyes opened slowly and then I saw dead bodies. After, I didn't think about any dead bodies, because for me myself, I am already dead. It is from there myself I come out my clothes. I took off my t-shirt and tie it around my stomach and crammed it in the hole in my stomach. Blood was filling my stomach, but the t-shirt stopped it running out. The blood stopped running, and I tried to come out the hole. The hole was so long, full of dead bodies. Some of them had white colours. Some of them had black colours.

I climbed the place up. It was up high, and I had to climb over it. It was about 1.5 metres deep for me to climb. I put my knee on top of the edge and after I came up, I looked down at the hole. I couldn't believe it. I saw all the dead bodies. It is still there now, today if I go to Libya, I will know that place. Even if they cover the dead bodies, I will know that place. I really know that place. I used to dream that place until I got to Europe. The place is far from the prison. But it is not far from the main road which is going directly to Zuwara. And that main road from Zuwara is going directly to Tunis. And the same main road, you can go to Algeria.

When I came out of the hole, I walked a small bit and then I fell down. I sat down on top of a fallen tree. After I get up, I walk and sit down again. After I get up the third time, I saw the main road. But you cannot describe the hole, because the hole is up and the main road is down the hill, and the hole is up the hill and then you come down again, so nobody will see it from the road. From the road you will see a hill, and on the other side of the hill there is a hole. There are no houses nearby, only desert. When you go so far you see the main road. And me, as I get to the main road, I fell down. I didn't know anything again, until I saw myself in the hospital.

I was lucky, but nobody ever explained that place. For Libyans, nobody know that place. For the people, that place that they throw people's children. Nobody know that they used to treat people. Some people don't die and they throw them in that hole, and they die there. Because they will not get any support to get out of there. As the people in there, their bones were all scratched, scratched. When they carry them, they throw them there and they will die. Me, I didn't have scratched bones, I only had stab wounds. That's why I had a chance to get out of there.

After I came out of the hole, I walk to the highway, and

I fell down. When I wake up, I see myself in the hospital. They now carry me to the hospital to the border of Algeria. The people who carried me in the main road, was one old man and a woman. They carried me to the hospital, and from there they carried me to the border of Algeria. I didn't see the guy who carry me to the hospital, I just woke up in the hospital.

When I wake in the following days in the hospital, I ask where I am. And the doctor responded, 'You are very lucky.' That was the border of Tunisia, Algeria and Libya. He said, 'You are very lucky, my friend. You have spent two days in a coma. We didn't know whether you would survive. Today you wake up. Two days. You are very lucky.' He explained how some people carried me here to the hospital. One old man and one woman.

So that old couple, they are Libyan travellers. That old man tell me he travelled plenty places you know. They used to go to Tunisia and Algeria all the time, so when they meet me, they bring me first to the Libyan border. From there, they carry me to the hospital, and they do the operation. All this is in the border. So the old man, he is passing by the hospital every time. He used to care about me. He used to come to the hospital, and he used to spend time with me. After he wanted to know who I am and what happened to me. Every time he used to pass, he would visit me in the hospital. It is like he did not want to leave me.

When I was in the hospital in Algeria, the doctors tell me that when they stopped the haemorrhage, they do their everything, they do the operation, and they take out dead blood. Because I run plenty hours and blood is not coming out, it was running inside of me. I tied my stomach with my clothes, that's why. The doctors told me that if I have my passport, this operation will not be in Algeria, it would be in Europe. So, as they saved me and made me to be in life, I should try to do my everything to have a better secure. Just to operate more. To do another operation. After I chat with the man, he asked me what I wanted to do. I said I want to go anyhow. He said that in Libya he had a house in Tripoli. He said he had friend that was working, building houses. And if I want, I can have his number.

I made my mind up. I must go back to Libya. So me, to my mind, it was not to be in Libya. I didn't mind Libya. Because me, I suffered in Libya, but for me now I know Libya, and I could now speak Arabic. I know what is going on in Libya. So I didn't think about Libya to stay. I was thinking about Europe, so that's why I go back to Libya, because if I go back to my house in my country, maybe I will not live long, because if I don't have this operation, it will disturb me more.

That time me, I want to go to Europe. That time me, I'm fed up. Because that time me, I don't have nowhere to go. I can't go back to my country, and I have problem. So for me, the only thing is, I will go up to the end. Whether I will die, or whether one day I will be alright. I want to go Europe because I want to have better cure. And that time themselves in the hospital, they used to say that if I have my papers, they would carry me in Europe to get a better operation. So the whole thing is me to go and get a better cure. So I said, this journey, I will continue in this journey, whether I die in the journey, whether I reach where I have good cure. That thing was in my mind. That's why I have the journey again.

Some people, when they meet me on the journey and they see my wound, they say me, I am mad. Some people are telling me, you are mad, you should go back. You are forcing yourself to go in this desert and Libya can only mean danger. The thing that I used to tell them is that if I go back home with this wound and with this problem, then maybe I will not live long because there is no good medicine and no good doctor who will cure me in my country. Because in Algeria, they have better doctors than in my country and they cannot cure me. So that's why I force myself. If I can reach, maybe I can reach. If I will die, then I will die, and everybody will forget about me. So I will rest in peace. That's why I continue, my friend.

The same old one who carried me to the hospital pick me to enter into Libya. In the time he was going on, so he made me like his worker. Like I am working for him doing masonry work. In the time I was going there, I didn't get myself have new clothes. I didn't make myself look as I have money. I buy material of working house, I buy masonry materials, I buy tools and I put them in the car. And I was dirty. I had dirty clothes because I was having one friend who was giving me that experience. You know. I was putting all dirty clothes and I travelling inside the car.

It was there on the way, we saw the police officers, they can drop us or the soldiers. Some people they can drop us. Because some people, they hate black people.* If you are

* In Libya, the life of a black migrant seems only worth what you can sell them for, the price of a mobile phone. Doro says that soldiers, police or 'some people' can 'drop us', pointing to the sheer lack of consequences for them of just shooting or killing black migrants.

going through to their country, you should be like a worker, or somebody who have been in their country for a long time, and go to do some work and come back. So that's why I put those dirty clothes and why I buy those materials for work. It is the system of the old man. Before, me I don't know that. They think I am a worker and I have been in Libya a long time, because I speak all Arabic.

When we go to Zintan, he drop me there with one of his friends who has plenty of houses to work. He has people who are working with his friends. He dropped me at his house. So he went back to Tripoli. That man is a good man, I didn't pay him nothing. Only God will pay him. He is a very good man. When I go to his house, because them two, they like somebody to be in their house to control their house, to clean their house, you know? To do the flowers and those things when they travel and I am working for his friends, and also I am in his house, so when they go travel, I stayed in the house, I cleaned the house, I do the things in the house. So, it was like that.

Today if those Libyan people saw me, they would not believe it because for me, all my friends who I had in the prison, I hear some people in Gambia, in Senegal. When they see me today, they used to talk to their friends in Libya and in Italy, when the friends tell them that I am in France, they never believe it.

One boy used to call me here. I saw him in Zuwara, the time that they sold us. He was one of the lucky ones who got taken on the bus to Tripoli. He was deported to Gambia. They told him that I am alive. He didn't believe it,

It is as though nobody cares. That's what he means when he so casually says 'drop us'.

until one day he got my number and called me. His name is Umar. He called me, he said 'Mo?'

I said, 'Yes.'

He said, 'Who are you?'

'It is me Mo, from Zawia.'*

He said, 'I never believed that you would be alive.'

Because they know the Ben Walid problem. The only people that I know that left Ben Walid alive are the ones who paid the money. Nobody else will make it alive. Nigerian women and men can sometimes get out.

Women, how they pay the money. You will see one Arab man who will come and pay for them to carry them out and carry them to his home. You will be there to sell yourself. A prostitute. Until you double the money. He will use you until then, and then he will get another woman to replace you. So then you will get your freedom. Then they are prostitutes and when they are free, they keep selling themselves until they have the money to cross.

And some people also. Boys. They escape Ben Walid, but they pay the money. Because the first time, when they give you the treatment, when they give you the phone, call your people, and they pay the money. Maybe you will be lucky. You will not face the treatment.

Doro felt as though he was lucky to have survived. I felt that luck is the reason why I have never faced such adversity. I have no idea what it is like to suffer in this way, and touch wood, I'll never have to find out. One thing that I've learned

* Most of Doro's friends call him Mo. It is short for Mohamad, and in the Serahule language, it means 'helper'. Doro is known by many friends in Libya and Europe as Mo.

over the last few years of helping people who have escaped from Libya is that the judgements of people back home don't really matter when you're sat next to someone who has been tortured. All I feel is empathy. So people can write what they want on social media, and make whatever judgements that they choose to, but until they can look someone like Doro in the eyes and say 'send them back', then maybe they should just stay quiet.

Doro had told me the most harrowing account of survival that I'd ever heard. I was left wondering how anyone could come through it at all, never mind be so assured and caring. Yet there he was, just telling me how lucky he felt to be alive. Then, as if he had said nothing at all, he stood up and walked to the kitchen asking if I wanted a drink or anything. I was dumbfounded by his account. 'Yeah, I'll have a beer, please pal.' I heard it hiss open in the kitchen and then he walked back smiling. I looked at him and thought what a hero he was just to survive all of this. He had shown me the scars as he spoke. I saw and felt some of the torment that he had endured. But here he was, cracking open a cold beer for me and sending me a warm smile, just to put me at ease, putting my feelings first.

I wondered what his thoughts were as to how he had made it so far. I asked him, 'Why do you think you survived?'

My best friend Ibrahim was sleeping in the prison. We slept together in the prison, side by side. We had been together for one year and six months. We had been in Tripoli together. He saved my life plenty of times. In the desert I go and collapse plenty of times because of water. It was getting small water. When he give a drink, he will save your life. So you will not give your water to anybody. But one day, he saved my life. He gave the water and he saved my life. And we walked again until we reached the city. He is why I am alive today.

And also the people who decided to carry me to one city in Algeria. First they took me to Zintan where they stopped the bleeding. But there was no good doctors there, they only stopped the bleeding. Then they carried me to Debdeb where I had my first operation, but I still had dead blood in my stomach, so they took me to another hospital. Name Illizi.* And I go to continue my operation. One month later I came out of the hospital. The doctors told me not to work for four months. But I cannot survive without working. In the months after I came out of the hospital I started to work to survive. Without no work I cannot survive. And I forget the operation and started to work hard. In some two months, I felt sick for the operation and started to shit blood. Because of the hard work I used to do started to disturb my stomach. For two months no help. I thought I would die. And I manage to come to be OK.

Moving on from the question I'd asked, Doro began describing the next stage of his journey. And that was fine by me . . .

I started to go to the old man's house in Libya and I stayed there for four months. I started to work for him. In a shop. I was arranging things in the shop. Sometimes the old man would leave me in the shop, and I worked throughout the

---

* Doro recounts this as though it is nothing, but he spent months in three different hospitals and almost died, a fact that he downplayed earlier, only surviving due to the kindness and generosity of his Libyan rescuers. He still suffers from this stab wound today.

day to sell things for him. I was very honest. I didn't take any risk because I wanted to repay him for my life. This old man is Libya people. The old man left everything to me, and I controlled the shop for four months. And the old man believed me and trusted me and gave me a place to stay. He was living with his three children and with his wife. I spent another six months in that house, making ten months and I decided to cross the journey again, because what I learned in Libya is that there are no human rights there. It is so dangerous. When they see a black man, they take him and sell him to the prison. After suffering, they carry him and follow him to die. I take taxi and go from the old man's house to go to a city called Sabratha.

Chapter 16

Second Attempt

At the checkpoint they arrest me and take me to the prison. They take everything. My phone and contacts and everything. After they take us from the prison where they took our everything, they put us in the camp. The prison and the camp are not the same. The prison is inside Sabratha, but the camp is far from the town, near the sea. After I went to the camp, they took my money as a tax for entering Sabratha, and they took me to a camp. That place is like a prison where they used to push people. It is occupied by a man called Mohamed Sabratha. He is the most wicked man in Sabratha. He is the man who controls Sabratha. He visit the camp three times a week. All the money is going to him. Everything we are paying after him pay the soldiers and him workers, everything is going to him account. He is a big man, I think. You see this man, every day that he come in the camp, the people who never pay, they will come out all of them, tied by their legs and tied by their hands and he will stand up. The man will start to beat everybody up to you make call. And when he beat you, he will say he will not be dirty. He would say in English, 'I will beat everyone. I don't want to be dirty. You people are black. You are all dirty. All blacks are dirty.' It was his words every time when he come in the camp.

In that camp, some people used to come from outside and come and take people to do jobs. Sometimes they would pay you and sometimes only food. So it is from there that I started to make small, small money. I used to go outside and buy cigarettes. Like big packets of cigarettes and come back and sell small, small, you know? I sell in the camp. I do plenty of business. Sometimes I go outside the camp, and I buy soap, food, chickens, from the money I have and come back and do business inside the camp.

The camp is far from the town. The camp is nearly to the water. It is a big place, but it is far from the town. And from the camp to the town there is big risk, because between the camp and the town you can have problems. They can kidnap you or go and sell you, or they will shoot you. But by that time the people who come and collect us to go and work, when they are coming back, they return us back to the camp, but it is that moment that me, I profit and I buy those things; chicken, cigarettes and come and sell it. It is there that I put money together, together and together and I have money. I stay in the camp so long until I have the money to go. This time I paid 1,500 dinar.

Plenty boys used to do that. They used to do plenty business. Some of them would wake up early in the morning and go to the town and buy things. That time all the Arab people are sleeping. Some people used to buy bread, plenty bread. They used to do plenty business, not only me. We do plenty things to make money.

Every pushing in Libya is night. This was at about 12 p.m. The weather was good and there were stars in the sky. It was a line of people. Every line is 10 people. And every boat took 110 people. Every line is controlled by three Arab people with gun. They will show you how to go down to the sea and enter in the water. When I was walking down to the boat, I did not get any bad thoughts as I know everything about the sea. If I get in a boat, I will enter Europe because I know the sea very well. I was getting hope as I walked down, but they took my chance.

When he start to the first line, he said 'Go'. Then he would walk to the last line he would say 'Go'. After he would come to the second line, and he would say 'Go'. So me, I didn't understand, I thought it would be first line then second line and so on. The man who was loading people inside the boat called for the next line. I didn't understand. I was in the second line, but I thought that when the first line went, the second line would go, but it was not this way. I was first to go in the second line, and when the first line went, I got up to run and follow. The Arab man just stopped me and hit me so hard that I fell down. I had lost my teeth.

The first knock, my teeth come out. I see my teeth where they fell down. I will never forget. I never took my teeth. After I ran to tell the main man Mohamed Sabratha. I rush to him and he started beating me with a rubber pipe. The other man was now vexed again and he hit me again to my eye with a Kalashnikov. When I fell down, I didn't get back up. I went unconscious until the following day. The people pick me up and take me to the place where we used to sleep, in the camp. It was a big house, so we slept until following morning, and we went to go back down.

The black man who carried me down, he said that now I should pay another money. The money for last night I lose. I said what about my eye, because that time my eye was big and my teeth had fell out.

I felt light-headed. My head was paining me. I told the Arab man that I go to the hospital. He said to me 'It's better that you die here than go to the hospital in Libya. No hospital will treat you because you are black.' It is hard as I would be back in that camp for three or four months before my eye calmed down. But after it calmed down, it started to become white like a cataract. So I started to be blind in my eye. My eye could not see anything, and my teeth were already down.

The man who do this is Baba. He has one leg. He is a slim guy. In the time of the fight, for the president Qaddafi, they say that the soldiers shot him in the leg. Then they took him to Italy to treat his leg. But in Italy they wanted to judge him, so he ran away to Germany, then he came back to Libya to work for the same man. That man is Mohamed Sabratha. They control Sabratha. Sabratha is in Libya, but it is in the west of Libya. It is a big city. It is only them that control there. Every black that wanted to cross in 2016/2017 they paid him. This happened in June 2017. In the July I didn't even get into the boat, but they took my money. If you pay the money, they take you to the seaside. If they don't push you, you lose your money. If you enter the sea, and you come back, you lose your money. That is the game. It is not only money, it is a game, it is luck. From the Arab people up to the seaside it is luck.

Chapter 17

Sabratha Camp

The camp in the seaside is called the white house. After my eye come well, I stayed in the camp for a small time. Like two months. A man looked after all of the camp. His name is Mohamed Baibul. Every end of the month, he used to organise everybody for the camp. He called everybody and tell them their rights.

'You, they push you. You never go. Your debt is expired. Your money is finished. I need only one more day for you to stay in my camp, after that you can go.' So, he used to come round.

If you know nothing outside the camp, they will catch you again and go sell you. If maybe you know some people in that place you can come out. Sometimes, if you get luck, you can come out of that place and find a better place to go work. You do an agreement with the man of the camp, Mohamed Baibul. You ask him; I want you to come carry me to go and work. Any work. When the work is finished, I want you to push me. Like me, that is what I did, but the people they never push them. He takes the people. They

are builders, construction workers. Inside they have plasterers for the inside. So as they go they explain to
Mohamed that they want to go. He wants to build one
house for his parents in Libya. They take them to the
workplace. They took me too. I signed the agreement and
go work there. But after the agreement he never went
through with his side. I worked until the house was finished. He came to push people. He just pushed the building
contractors. He left the people there. It is then when I
decided to leave there and go to Zuwara.

He wasted my time. He ate my money. And he showed
me wickedness. Because of that man, we worked for his
house, until we built his house for over six months and
then he came and took a few people and pushed them. And
he left some people, and he came and said to the others
that he will push them the next time. And that time will
never come. Even if the next time comes that he pushes
people, he will push other people other than you. And
leave you there until the next time, until the next time and
the next time, until everything you delete.*

You will not work to get money. You will stay there eating what they give you. And you never go travelling like
you expected to do. That was my journey, it was very
complicated. After I come out of there, I decided to come
out on my own because I was seeing friends who used to
bring business inside the camp, like cigarettes. Inside the
camp, we can sell it. Outside the camp, we can buy cigarettes for ten and sell it inside the camp for twenty. So
some Arab man, they go outside the camp and they bring

* Doro means that he will slowly take one thing from you at a time,
until you are left with nothing, not even your life.

me the things to sell for them. After a while I spoke to my friend who used to give me the cigarettes to sell, and he got his car. I explained to him that I didn't pay my boat. I am here in the camp. I work for the main man, who said he will push us, but still he never pushed us. And people come and meet me, they go and enter Europe, but still I am here. So I didn't get money. So I want to go and hustle. He now told me that there is only one place in Libya where I can go and work and they will pay me, no problem. Where the people are not wicked. Where there is law. He said to go to Zuwara.

I asked how will I get to Zuwara, and he told me that he can take me there, but when I start to work, I must pay him back. This way I will take you from this camp. Because in that camp they will lock you in the camp. In the morning they guard the gates for you to come out, someone will come to the gates to say that they carry you to go work. Because they don't want you to come out and explain to people what is happening in that camp. So the man came to the gates, he talk to the guards. He talked to them, and they called me. I entered into the car, and he dropped me in Zuwara. As he dropped me, he dropped me at a house, Piesta, they pushed us. It is there that the taxi driver dropped me.

Doro had not told me about this part of his journey when I was in France with him. There was perhaps so much to say. There were often areas where I would have to call him to get more information. I sat at my kitchen table most times, recording telephone conversations with him, trying to piece together what had happened. These interviews were the most difficult because they were recorded telephone conversations, being made between shifts at work, having to coordinate time when Doro was free, and all without the personal touch of being in the same room as one another. Nevertheless, we managed to piece together the story, going over specific details again and again. I wanted to be there to read his body language. It was hard to tell when a moment was difficult for him to relive. The psychological trauma of his time in Libya is tangible, encrypted in the strain of his voice, or with the saddening of his eyes as he drifted into memories. Sometimes I could feel that he was scared to remember. I tried never to pressure him, but I wish that I'd been able to do more of the interviews and piecing together of the story when I was with him in France. The next chapter was mainly recorded during our time together in Bourges.

Chapter 18

Third Attempt

I was in Zuwara for seven or eight months. I was working for that big mosque, Jama Kabil. When we was working in the big mosque, we found contacts to pay so we could cross again, so we pay, me and my friend. Zuwara was a good place because there was not any fighting. There was not war at the time. There was not political thing. So that place, when you work, they will pay you. So after I worked I saved to pay. It was 1,500 dinar we pay to the smuggler, 2,000 to the pusherman.

When I was working, I meet people I know. Those plenty people, they call them pushermans. In Libya there are plenty black people whose work only is to pushing people; they are finding customers for Arab people. Only blacks can do that job. If Arab man come to me and say that they know an Arab man who will push and you will bring money, you will not give it to him. Because when the Arab man eat your money, no problem, you cannot do nothing. So now they will take black mans to work with them and say that they have one Arab man who used to push. If you want to go, I will write your name, you will pay your money and I will tell him that you want to go. So the day of pushing he will call you and you will come. So after I see one man, he is from Mali. He say he works for one Arab man, he is a good man. He is used to pushing people; called Ali. So then Ali push us. He is still pushing today. Even tomorrow he is pushing. He is an ex-soldier.

The night they come to push us in Zuwara, It is not far from the water. So they carry us in one place where they used to make the oil. It is like a camp. It was a big oil company, but now it is abandoned. Nobody is working in that oil company. It is an old oil company. They took us to this old factory. It was an old house. They call us and everybody must go to this one garage, Piesta garage. He will grab you people, four or five people in a taxi, other taxi, four and five people, and other taxi – it will work like that, and small van, and he will carry us into the old, abandoned factory. So you will sit down and wait for the Arab man to come. When the Arab man come, he will count all the people and count the money. There were a hundred-and-something people. But the man, plenty people were not trusting him. Because they said that he pushed once and he never succeeded. So we say that we will try. But he have a hundred-and-something people in that pushing.

When they come with the boat they come and take some people, the tough people, to come and make the boat. After some people we go and make the boat. When we make the boat, from there they call everybody, and we come and carry the boat and put it inside the water. After, we come one by one and enter inside the boat, because they don't like people to rush. When people rush you can get problem even before the boat move.

The boat is chest height, and you climb into the back of it and then go to the front and sit down. If there was a young boy, they will carry him on the shoulders and drop him on the boat. If you are fit, you will carry the small boys. Then the smuggler comes to start the engine. He brings a speedboat up to the big boat, so everybody is inside the big boat. He enter into the big boat and walks over the top of everybody to get to the back of the boat. He started the boat. Started it again. Then he drive the boat up for fifteen minutes to get us away from the beach. After, they bring their speedboat and the smuggler man left our boat and entered the speedboat and tell you good luck. And he goes back to Tripoli.

We had a compass. Like a telephone. We go up until the morning. They gave us a compass bearing to aim on. We didn't see any risk. The compass will be beside twenty-five to thirty [bearing] and four knots. So we run up to the morning. Some people are saying we reach international water. Some people are saying no, we never reach. We could see no land. Nothing. Just the sea. We were just in the middle of the Mediterranean.

After some time, the captain said we were talking too much, and he turned off the engine to speak. After he turned off the engine, the engine would not start again. The captain took off the top of the engine to fix it, but he could not make it work. The engine never started. After a while we saw a fishing boat and he came. He is a Libyan. He asked us where we are going to. We said we are going to Italy. He said international is too far; you people are still in Libyan water so it is not secure for you to stay here. So he said, 'You people give us the bad engine, and we will give you our small engine and you will be able to use it.'

He said that the small engine will take us to international waters. The captain agreed with him and took off the engine. We first gave him our engine, before he give us the other engine, but then the fisher boat left with both engines and tell us bye bye.

Doro started laughing at how the man was waving to them as he drove away with their engine, leaving them in the middle of the sea with no sight of land, no food or water, and no engine. He mimicked the way that he looked behind him, smiling at his own impersonation of the man who left them for dead. Doro's nonchalance at being left in this way and his ability to laugh at the cruelty that they faced will always amaze me. He bears no malice towards the people who took the engine. That's just the way it was. In fact, it is the same way that, as a rescuer, I've heard many people describe to me. The 'engine fishers', as we call them, have an industry of collecting the used engines from the rubber boats and taking them back to Libya to sell. As rescuers, we realised this, so we started to take the engines from the boats after the rescue, to stop them being used again. Then, they started to take the engines even before the rescue. The recklessness of this is staggering. I'll always be bewildered as to how one person could leave another in the sea, facing possible death, without an engine, just for a few dollars. Life is cheap, but in Libya and in the sea away from Libya, life seems to be worth nothing at all.

It was 12 o'clock in the daytime. We saw Libyan Marines, they are coming. When the guy take our engine, I thought that we were dead. Everybody was crying thinking we will not see again the outside, because we are in the tip of the water. No engine, no food, no nothing. So we were so confused. Up until 12 o'clock, we were so confused. But the weather was good. We had luck. The water was not spoiling. A big ship coming to us with two small ships. Like you people when you rescue us.

Some people thought we were in international waters. That they were people coming to rescue us. Some people said that they recognised the big boat, it is Italy. Some people say it is Malta. Some people say it is Spain and it went like this. Then they come up to us and I saw the flag of Libya, and I say no – this one is the Marines. They take us to the prison. They caught us and took us to the big ship and back to Libya. When they caught us, I knew the prison and I said that I could not go to the prison. That time I was saying that this thing will be more than anything.

They came with small boats and dragged our boat away. They gave us a rope and dragged us up to the big ship and dropped a cargo net to our boat. We had to climb up.

Chapter 19

Zuwara

They bring us in Zuwara. Immigration. After, they carry us to Zintan immigration camp. Where I was before. The big man in Zintan is Nigel. Him brother name is Ali. I went to their house to work. From the people, they picked me and Adam Rasta.

After we come to the immigration camp, we stayed for two weeks. They bring the big trucks to carry people to deporting. And that deporting this time is not deporting by plane. They will carry you to La Saba, and then you will go to Agadez. It is by road. But me and Adam, we have luck. They come and everybody, they introduce you and they take Adam because he said that he worked masonry. I said also that I knew masonry, so they took all the other people for deporting. By that time the contractor a big builder called Mohamed. He buy plenty cement. All the cement is spoiling and he didn't have people to build the house, so he took me and Adam to stay and work for him. In the morning he come straight to our house, and he asked, 'You people are builders?'

I said, 'Yes.' So he said, 'I will have you work in my house and build the fence.'

We built twenty small rooms for the people working in the immigration centre for the new people that they recruit there. And he said we will work for him for six or seven months and after, we asked for the money and he started to give us problems. So we go to La Saba. Because we know that he will not pay us. The contractor look at us and we are blacks, and he don't want to pay us. But we work seven months from six in the morning to seven in the evening.

The man I was working with is an old man, Adam. Nearly fifty years old. He said he had two daughters in Ghana. After we go back, we go back to La Saba. People need masonry workers there. We worked there two weeks. In the third week, Adam didn't wake up. I call the Imam. They took him to Zawia hospital. They said that he died.

After the hospital, the landlord asked if I would continue to work. I said that I cannot work without Adam as he is the number one. He said he had friends in Sabratha and I can work for them. So he went and dropped me in Sabratha, but that time Sabratha has war. We couldn't stay. So he now tells me that we should leave this place. So he asked me where I wanted to go, and I know Zuwara so I asked him to take me back to Zuwara. He now tell me that he cannot enter me in Zuwara so he took me back to La Saba. At the time people from La Saba cannot go to Zuwara because of the war, so he took me to a taxi place. The taxi take me to Bangala house in Zuwara.

Chapter 20

Bangala House

And that house, I was somebody who bring people there, because when I first got there it was not somewhere for blacks. I only knew that there were six or seven blacks. And then I started to work. And when I saw blacks in the streets, and I talked to them, I would find out that they were paying a lot of rent. And that house, I was paying a small amount of money each month. The man who owned the house, had a shop inside. The shop is giving him money, so the house was not comfortable. He just built a small house. So I started to invite people. After I started to find people to get more information to get the journey for how to cross, I meet one Senegalese man. He spoke the same language as me. His name was Bubacar. I started to be friends. He explained everything to me about the journey. He was working for one Arab woman, taking bags of sand and carry it on his head and take it up in the building site to the second, third, fourth floor. This is why he is still sick in Romania now. We stayed together in Zuwara. Now I worked with him to be a builder. He is my helper. And we work in Zuwara until I get money to cross, me and Bubacar.

Our eyes connected when he mentioned Bubacar and straight away, Doro started smiling at me from his chair. It was early into the evening, and we'd just eaten a Senegalese dish of lightly spiced rice, mixed with peas and chicken. This was real friends' talk, without him showing any of the fear of his memories. His voice was almost joyous. Doro was happy just at the thought of his friend. Bubacar was one of the forty-seven people that we'd rescued in the sea. It became apparent after a few days of sailing together that many of the people on the ship already knew each other. Bubacar was a quiet thoughtful man with an infectious, blanket-warm smile, who loved to sit and talk with the younger guests on the ship, explaining to them about the world, the political situation on the ship, and reassuring the others that everything would be alright in the end. He didn't take part in the fitness classes or the football, and at the time I thought nothing of it. Looking back, knowing what I now know about Bubacar, maybe the physical strain of his ordeal was the reason for him not taking part.

Bubacar was so kind, I can see. He tell me he is born in Kaolack in Senegal, but he do everything in Gambia, so he is Senegal-Gambia like me. I was so proud of him. He showed me the better journey and I started to believe him. So one day I was looking for people to start a job. I was finding a helper and I had to carry the bags. It is a hard job. And they will not pay you much money. After my first day I chatted with Bubacar. We come down, the Arab man paid us, and Bubacar asked me where I was living. I said Bangala house. I asked him where he was living. He said he is living in another place. And I asked him how much he was paying. He was paying a lot more than me, so I told him to come and live with us in Bangala.

The house in Bangala just came with nothing. No furniture or beds, so we used to find the things that people had thrown away. Everything that they threw, mattresses, covers and everything, and we would bring it to the house, so that when people come, they can sleep. After, the man who owned it respected me. He left me in the house to manage it. He respected me and come to be my friend. After his younger brother knew a pusherman and it is that man who pushed us, and after, you people come to rescue us.

Bubacar is kind. He is a tall man and knows how to make it. The time we were working, some people who were working, they got money and went to find girls, prostitutes to pay, and go and drink. But not Bubacar. Bubacar likes to smoke. He smokes too much, one packet a day. But he is very serious. He is always on the phone to his family. He got one problem with an Arab woman there. He said that the Arab man didn't pay him for his work, and the Arab man accused Bubacar of stealing his phone. But I know Bubacar would never steal. For me though, he was foolish. You cannot argue with the Arab man in Libya.

We became best friends, and we lived together in the house. Because everybody in the house, they know me. Like the king of that house. If you say 'Mo', everybody will know me. If you get a problem, they will donate it to me. The man in the shop was going every day. Blacks they are buying – everybody is buying from him. Sometimes, I used to be told that it was not necessary for me to pay rent because I filled Bangala house with dozens of people.

Bubacar knew everybody. And we had friends. Ismail

was my friend there. Ibrahim* I knew also. Nobody spent
more time in Zuwara prison than him. He was there for
more than two years. But he was an informant. He cannot
be my friend because he used to inform on the blacks. After
I brought him to Bangala house, people used to recognise
him. But I used to say, 'It was not Ibrahim who used to give
the treatments. That was the days of the prison. Let us put
those days behind us. You must not fight each other. Find
your destination and look after each other. It is better than
to fight. In this house, there is no fighting.'

I controlled Bangala house like my own father's home.
And Arab people respected me, because now I can do anything. I was getting power in Zuwara because the owner
of the house is a big military man in Zuwara. Since the
time of Qaddafi. He gave me power in the house. If there
were any problems in the house, they would call me and
explain, and I would tell him. He took the money from the
families and bring them from the prisons and take them to
Bangala house. People started to call me Mo. It means
helper. That's why I got that name.

All my time I spent in Zuwara I spent in Bangala. The
time I first came to Bangala house, there was six people.
By the time I left there were more than 250 people. And all
of those people wanted to cross. We paid the man and the
man tell us to stay until the end of the month, as the
weather is too bad. At the end of one month the sea will
be OK. Now the weather is not good. And we believed
him. After another month, the man called us and direct us
to the Arab man, and the Arab man carry us. We was fifty

* A different Ibrahim from his best friend who had died in Bani
Walid.

people in the sea boat, but the water was not good for us. That was Thursday. The Arab man now tell us that he cannot push us as the sea is not 100 per cent. The sea is bad in international, and he didn't push us that day. The following day he came and said that he will push us in the night. We left around 3 a.m.

And all of those people I left in Bangala, and I hear in the news that they are in prison. And some I hear the news that they died. I know plenty people who were on the boat that you people see the day before you rescued me. They were in Bangala. Plenty of them, they come out in front of us and they push them. It is that very day that they wanted to carry us too. But they didn't push us. They pushed the other people and they all died.

The people that you see dead in the sea, we were together in Bangala house. But it was not the same Arab man who did the push. Our Arab man said he will not push that day, because his father said let him not push that day. But the other Arab man collected the people in Bangala. And some of them were my friends. Some of them were from Guinea Bissau.* The pusherman asked me if I wanted to come with him and take me with that boat, but I didn't go.

At the time that Doro was waiting to be sent to sea, I was on the *Sea-Watch 3*, the only NGO ship in the search and rescue zone at the time, patrolling a vast amount of sea, from north of Al Khoms in the east of Libya, to north of Zuwara and Sabratha in the west. It's a very large area of sea for us to patrol, and it's impossible for us to patrol effectively with just

* At this point, Doro started saying their names.

one ship. On the evening of 17 January 2019, we were patrolling in the western side because the weather conditions at
sea looked better in the west, making it an area where the
smuggler would be more likely to send boats. These predic-
tions are near impossible to make as each smuggler has a
different appetite for risk, and the situation between the war-
ring militias on land is difficult for us to predict also. We have
to make a best guess, usually by looking at the weather and
the size of the waves at sea. These are the only factors that
we can understand from the ship, but the factors on land are
completely unpredictable.

Doro spoke of 120 people who were sent to Al Khoms to
leave, and fifty people who were due to leave from Zuwara. We
were patrolling north of Zuwara, 16 hours from the other side
of the search and rescue zone that day. Late in the evening we
were alerted to a report of 120 people on a rubber boat north
of Al Khoms. The boat was sinking and there were already
people seen in the water. An Italian helicopter had found them
and reported that they'd dropped two life rafts into the sea.
The helicopter had winch-rescued three people from the wreck
and was taking them back to Italy.

It was our worst-case scenario. We were right on the other
side of the search and rescue zone, hours to the south-west of
them. We sailed in their direction, knowing that we'd be too
late, but also knowing that for some, there may be a small
chance that they could hold onto something. A chance to save
a life is not something we're going to ignore. Other ships were
closer, but we knew that few of them would want to respond.
Matteo Salvini, the then Deputy Prime Minister of Italy, had
seen to that. He had been trying to discourage and to criminalise the people who rescued those leaving Libya. Any ship that
rescued people was threatened with prosecution. The cargo

vessels knew that they wouldn't be allowed into their ports. Other cargo ships that had rescued people had already been made an example of. Even an Italian coastguard vessel was blocked by their own home authorities. Humanitarian rescue had been made toxic and dangerous. It is something that I still cannot fathom. It led to us knowing that this sinking boat would most likely be ignored. We might be their last hope, we'd never know. We just had to go.

Kim woke us up late in the night to call us for a meeting. He'd been told, to our surprise, that a cargo ship was responding to them, but also that it might not be able to rescue them due to the size of the ship. We were most of the way there by then, so we just kept going. We spoke about salvaging the dead, about searching for the living. We got there in the very early hours of 18 January 2019. Two RHIBs were dropped into the water to start the search. Rob drove the first one and found the first life raft. I heard him on the radio saying that there was nobody in it. I drove the other RHIB looking for the other raft.

The search wasn't easy as it was quite windy and cloudy, making the sea as black as the sky, without even a star to light the way, and with the waves pitching the RHIB about a bit, looking for signs of life was really slow. In the end, we found the second life raft and looked inside. Nothing. Then we searched around the area for a while, finding pieces of the rubber boat, the transom, a pack of cards, shoes. Cigarettes, papers, clothes, and a few small possessions were all that we could find, eerily floating around in the blackness, marking the spot where the boat went down. After three hours of searching, no bodies had been found, alive or dead. News outlets in the following days reported that 117 people had drowned, including ten women and two children, one of which was a two-month-old baby.

Doro

It was horrific to circle around looking for their bodies knowing that below the waves so many people had drowned. What was so disheartening was the sheer needlessness of it all. Of course, in the most militarised sea on the planet, there are plenty of government navy vessels that can and should have been able to respond. In fact, just two years earlier, there was a European naval operation to do just that, but the European policy makers decided to shut it down, leaving just the NGOs to save lives. Then the NGOs were targeted, with so many ships confiscated by the authorities on spurious charges and investigations that were just designed to tie the ships in red tape. This all manifested itself in the removal of rescue vessels, and us being the only ones in the search and rescue zone, and we simply can't be everywhere. If only there had been another ship that we could have coordinated with, we would have sent one to the east, whilst we stayed in the west, covering as much area as possible. Instead, we guessed that the most likely departure point would be in the west. We were wrong.

Chapter 21

Fourth Attempt – Boza

I was sitting in my house with some of my friends drinking lemon tea. The Arab man came to my door and said it is time to go. He sent a car with a driver to start carrying people to the seaside. It was a long Mitsubishi van, nine people at a time. And soon he transported all the people. There were fifty people taken to the seaside. But three people were left. I don't know why they couldn't go. I just saw that we were all kept in a room by the sea, like a tourist place. Like a place where people would come in the summertime. He came and called some people. The Arab man comes to us and he say that he cannot push all of us, that three will not come. And they were from Nigeria. He said that they were not 100 per cent. So they took forty-seven people.

He made sure that there was a captain, and a compass man. As he called me and Ibrahim, he carried us down to the sea, and then he put all the engine and the boat by a bush there. The boat was new. We built the boat and laid it on the ground, putting the wood where they were supposed to be and inflated the boat following the directions. It only took an hour. After we finished everything, we carried the fuel. He asked the captain how many gallons he needed. The captain said that he needed ten gallons. I said, 'No, let him give us twenty or twenty-five.' Ibrahim said, 'Why are you getting involved? You are not the captain.' I said, 'No, but I have experienced the sea.' So the man gave us twenty-five gallons. After, I saw the crew coming. Because the man trusted me after he saw how I was able to build the boat. Even the time he was showing the captain the engine, the captain didn't know about the key. He thought he would just pull the engine and it would go. He came to me and asked, 'Do you know how to work this engine?' I said, 'Yes, it was my work as a fisherman.' He then got into the boat and started the engine.

The man called the pusherman and asked why he didn't tell him that I could drive the boat. I said that I paid for the journey, not to drive the boat. I didn't earn all this money to come to Europe as the driver, because if they saw me as the captain, they could lock me in the prison. So I just wanted just to pay to cross. Then, all of us we come. We stood all round the boat. And some people took the gallons of fuel. And some of us started to pray. *Bismillah ilahija halla*. It means peace be to God. God is the merciful one.

So we carried the boat on our shoulders like the first time. We put the boat in the water and one by one we climbed in. The captain was first in, and the man explained to him how to work the engine. And then the compass man. They explained to him how to work the compass. Everybody climbed on to the boat, and after, the man gave someone a satellite telephone to call for a helicopter. He gave out his number so that if there was a problem we could call. After, he climbed into the boat and turned on the engine. The man drove the boat a small way. And then got back on to the other boat to take him back and off we go.

We left at three in the morning, but the captain was not going anywhere. The boat was just going around in circles. And he was struggling, and eventually the boat managed to go forwards. The man who drive the boat didn't know how to drive the boat; he drive it in circles. He didn't know left and he didn't know how to go right, and the boat was in a circle in the deep sea. So I took the boat because I save my life. Because I knew I can do it. Before, I was a fisherman, so now I tell the boys, the man, you cannot drive the boat. You risk our lives. You enter into the boat. And even the compass man didn't know how to compass.

In Libya you can take the boat if you tell the smuggler that you know how to drive the boat. Everybody was stressed. Nobody knew what to do. They were insulting the man who was the captain: 'If you did not know how to drive this boat you should not have said it. You are risking our lives. You are going to kill us.' Someone else would be shouting: 'Turn back, we want to go back. You're going to kill us. You don't know nothing!' Everybody was complaining. So I calmed everyone down. I said, 'Let's calm down. It's not that he didn't know how to drive the boat. He knows how to drive, but maybe he is confused. Give him a chance. Maybe he can drive us.'

After everyone calmed down, I came in front of him, and told him how to work the machine. I explained to him how to drive the boat. But still after a long while, it was clear that he was driving it too heavy-handed. He was starting to damage the boat by turning it too much in the waves. It was a nylon boat, and the tubes can cut. It's not necessary to drive it fast. You turn it small, small, and then turn the engine up slowly.

I kept trying to explain to him, but he could not get it. So I told him to push. And everybody started to laugh. I said, 'Me, I paid for the boat. I did not take driving, but I took the boat to save our lives. They pay you to drive the boat, but me, nobody pay me. I just want to save our lives. But anybody in the boat here. If you want, we can all die. Me, I already died. I will drive the boat and we shall reach Italy Inshallah. If I don't drive it, we will die. But anybody they ask you in Italy who drive the boat, if you tell them it is me who drive the boat, you will get problem in the spirit. Because I am saving your life.' It is the agreement we make.

After a while, we made a phone call. We spoke to a woman in England. It's an emergency number that we called, and we gave them our direction. After a small time after the telephone call, we saw the aeroplane over our heads. The people that we called, said to give our directions, and while we were talking to them on the phone, we saw the aeroplane. After, the phone was thrown into the sea.

There are lots of organisations which help the people making this journey. Often the people are criminalised by politicians or in the press, but there is an important distinction between these rescue organisations and the smuggling networks. Talk of collusion between the NGOs and the smugglers is utterly misplaced. Alarmphone is an organisation which has people in Europe ready to coordinate a rescue. Plasterers, nurses, students, teachers – ordinary people who know the dangers at sea give their own time to run a self-organised call centre which people can ring. They'll then contact the appropriate coastguards giving details of the boats' locations, and then make sure that they do their job, and effect a rescue.

There are also NGOs with reconnaissance planes that search the area for boats in distress, and organise to effect their rescue, giving details of the locations, directions of travel and their speed. Then there are organisations like Sea-Watch who use boats to patrol the search and rescue zone and respond to distress calls. Often it is very difficult to either contact the various coastguards, or to get them to respond to the distress calls appropriately. It seems that every government going is trying to pass the responsibility of rescue. Meanwhile, people like Doro float in the sea, in the most dangerous of conditions, on over-crowded, flimsy rubber boats, with no life-jackets, no lights, and with few people caring whether they live or die.

When I saw the aeroplane, I told everybody that we were in international water. I didn't say that we were rescued. I just told them that we must be in international water. Because, on my first journey I saw the aeroplane and then I was still in the prison. So I had to be cautious. When I saw the aeroplane, I knew that we were so far from Libya, that we would be in international water. I explained to everybody how the colour of the water be a deep blue, so I knew we must be in international water. And we saw dolphins racing under the boat.

After I told them that we were out of Libyan water, everybody started to be happy. People were waving at the aeroplane. We saw two aeroplanes. A big one, and a small one. The first plane that saw us did a big circle around us.

We were waving and calling to them. And then it went back. Then it came back and turned around us and went again. And then a third time it came and did a circle around us, and then it went, and we didn't see it again.

The other big plane come, and everybody started shouting, 'Help us, help us.' After, we saw a big ship in front of us. It was a fishing boat. It was a big fishing boat. The small aeroplane came back and went straight back in the same direction, so we followed it. Some people were saying that we should go to the fishing boat, but I said no, we should follow the plane. After an hour I followed the fishing boat, but it was not stopping for us. We went for thirty minutes and then we could see water splashing in the sky on the horizon. It was a boat coming at us with speed. It was far away, and we couldn't hear it, but just see it on the horizon.

I told the people on the boat, 'This one is a Libyan boat. We are in big trouble', because I could see that it was a fast boat like the Libyans have. Some people were saying that they would jump to the water and drown before they get taken to Libya. I don't want to go to prison. I said also that I don't want to live again in Libya, and I knew that I would drown myself before I let that happen. And everybody was scared. Everybody went quiet. Nobody was talking. We were so scared. After, we could see you were coming and now, we started to see.

Bubacar said it first. 'Doro, this does not look like Libyan. Look at this man. He does not look like an Arab.' Still nobody dared to be happy. And when we saw you coming close, we slowed down. Up until we hear you speak nobody really knew. Then we hear you shouting, 'Hello, we are from Europe, you are safe now!' Everybody was happy. We were celebrating, shouting Boza, Boza, Boza. We knew it was Europe because nobody from Libya would greet us by saying that we were safe.

Doro stood up from his chair wearing the biggest smile as he relived the moment that they were found. Boza means freedom.

It was like you took everything in life and every good thing and you put it in my heart. I just thought: Oh My God! I was so happy. I get so emotional; I cannot explain it. I was so happy, that I didn't know what to do because after I saw myself, I saved myself, you know. And after you said that we will go to Europe. And after you said that we are safe. That moment, I will not forget it. Everybody was happy. The happiness makes you cannot stand. And nobody knew what to do. Everybody was full of happiness.

And after a moment you started to organise us. And you told us to follow you, but the captain had turned off the engine. And soon the captain would not drive the boat, and there was an argument. But nobody dared to be the one to be seen to be the captain. And soon everybody calmed down, and you started to give us lifejackets, and took us to the big ship. The time that you rescued us, there were many boats going into the Mediterranean and some people died. Some people were taken back and some in the prison. The time that you rescued us, it had been a long time that nobody had made it to Europe because Italy closed the border.

For us there was no rescue boat in the sea. We did not think that we would be rescued by Europe. That's why

I demanded twenty-five gallons. It was Malta, Lampedusa, or death. I said that there is no rescue in the sea, we must find Malta or Lampedusa, or we will die. I knew that with this much fuel, that I would see Malta or Lampedusa, and if we did not, we would die. But now I know that it was impossible in that small boat.

'Europe or death' is a phrase that we commonly hear on the ship. Doro didn't say it quite that way, though. He said that they would hit Malta, Lampedusa or that they would die. Their desperation to leave Libya and start a new life in safety, and with a future in which they can maybe flourish, means that people like Doro head out to sea without any real idea of what it will be like on the way, or how dangerous it is, or in fact that it is such a long way. Once they hit the high seas, the waves can fold the boards in the bottom of their dinghy causing the boards to separate and create small holes in the rubber tubes, causing their boats to deflate and sink, with no rescue plan, and nothing to hold on to. Few of them can even swim.

At that time, the *Sea-Watch 3* was the last remaining NGO vessel at sea. The others had all been stopped, blocked, or were under investigation. Each time, having to take governments to court to allow them to sail. If Proactiva had not been blocked, if *Sea-Eye* were allowed to sail, or the *Lifeline*, or the *Iuventa*, or any of the rescue ships that had been removed from the sea, then we could have worked together to make sure that as much of the sea as possible was covered.

The insanity of it was just incredible. Here we had fully crewed and equipped rescue boats, ready to go to the aid of drowning people, real human beings like you and like me, and the governments were doing everything that they could to stop them. They were consciously and maliciously removing any help for the people at sea by hook or by crook. They were simply tying us in red tape.

On 22 December 2018, the *Sea-Watch 3* rescued thirty-two people. It was the mission before we'd found Doro. They had sailed to Malta and were waiting outside the ports asking for permission to bring them in. Matteo Salvini had said that they would not be allowed into Italy, and the Maltese authorities were denying them entry there too. On 5 January 2019, my mission began by taking over from the old crew outside the port of Valletta. The old crew were all allowed to land, the people that they'd rescued were not. It was not until 9 January 2019 that we were able to disembark them. In those days, I was helping to teach a one-year-old to walk. There were little kids playing on the life rafts, packed away on the rear deck. I sat and drew pictures with them, sang songs and wrestled. It was just too incredibly inhuman to leave them at sea like that, but that was Europe's new humanity. It was two small children like those on our ship who drowned amongst the 117 on 18 January 2019 – a cruelty for which Europe is directly responsible.

Returning people to Libya is a contravention of refugee law, as it is the law to take the people to a safe port. It would be illegal to take them anywhere else. When cargo ships, NGOs and even Italian coastguard ships have rescued people, their ships have been denied entry into the safe ports. Imagine the dilemma of some of the big cargo ships who could help. On one hand, they are duty-bound to rescue the people. On the other, they know that if they do so, they will be denied entry to safe ports, thereby losing thousands of euros for each day that they are kept at sea. Eventually, many of them have decided not to rescue at all. So the civilian cargo ships ignore the calls for help, the military vessels have pulled out and the Libyan coastguards don't even answer their phones.

For months and months, the status quo became an arbitrary political waiting game. Each time an NGO ship rescued people, Italy and Malta would tell them that they could not come. The rescue ships would be faced with little choice but to head to the closest European country and ask for permission to land, which would be immediately denied. They then had to wait for the political manoeuvring to conclude before eventually being allowed in. Then the investigations would begin in order to stop or delay them from going back to rescue more people. Politicians in Europe would demand that we take the people back to Libya, but to do so would contravene the 1951 refugee convention, whereby it is illegal to take people back to the country from which they are escaping. We were the only ones keeping to the law, and we were being criminalised for it.

For Doro and the other forty-six people that we'd rescued, it meant that there would be a prolonged period for us to wait together whilst the politicians bickered over who should take the people that we had rescued. It was a cruelty that I cannot overstate. These victims of torture and abuse, and some victims of war, were exercising their legal and human right to try to escape. They were physically and mentally exhausted, from both the journey that they had taken and from years of abuse before. I spoke to some who said that staying on the ship for an indefinite length of time felt like they were being imprisoned. It was awful, but we did what we could to pass the time and make them feel welcome.

Chapter 22

Ship Life

After finding the rubber boat that Doro and the others were on, we towed them towards the ship. Slowly and carefully, we shuttled them from their little blue dingy onto the *Sea-Watch 3* using the rescue RHIBs. I stretched out with a knife, cutting the rubber tubes of their little boat so that it could never be used by the smugglers again and watched as it submerged into the water. We then climbed up onto the deck of the ship where there were jubilant scenes. Our new friends were hugging each other and thanking the rest of the crew. As we climbed up, some of them came to thank us for rescuing them. We attended to their medical needs and sat them down at the back of the ship, where they would stay until we were able to disembark somewhere safe. I wanted to capture Doro's feelings of this time before I left to go back home, where future interviews would be much more difficult. It was around midnight. His balcony window was open and fresh air was blowing into the room.

The first night on the big ship I remember thinking how I was safe now. I was so happy; it came through me. After you rescued us, I remember that you showed us on a map where we had come to. Even with 100 gallons we would not have made it to Europe. Because the water is not good, in that weather.

The first night I slept and I waked up and I could see that I was on the ship, and you people were all around me. I was praying to God. Thanking God and thanking the people for saving our lives. I was so happy. Even if Italy didn't like to take us, then I am OK. And that time, even if I had died, I'm OK, because I realised that I needed to be rescued. And now everybody is in peace and thank Sea-Watch. And thank God. And thank all you people. May God give you a long life.

The life on the ship was another experience for me. It was beautiful. Some people didn't know what it was like on a ship. They had never been on the water. They didn't know the test of water. And what water was. I used to smile and know what the colour of it is. As we were inside the sea, I experienced a lot from people. For some people, maybe they are thinking that we will not come down to Italy. Even me. I asked you if one day you will take us back to Libya. You said, 'No. Never!' and I understand.

For plenty of people they thought like that. Like if Italy didn't accept. Like how Lampedusa said no, and then Malta. And then we were outside Italy, and they were saying no. Lots of us were so scared that if Italy and all of Europe said no, then soon you would take us back to Libya. Me, I thought that if they take me back, I will throw myself off the ship and drown in the sea. Because I know where I came from. I spent many years there. I know the hardness.

And the Sea-Watch we stay fifteen days with them. Everybody was happy. No big stress. And every time advice with them. And they are like fathers to us, brothers, sisters, and real friends. I never see better friends in my life, and I would not believe in Europe until I will die, I will see those kind of friends and the help that they used to give us.

And inside the sea, I experienced something about food. Some people were complaining about the food. Some people were saying that they were not full and the toilet was full. But me, I knew that the boat was better than where we had come from. They were safe. Nobody would be shooting them if they went to the wrong place. Sometimes I had to tell people that the Sea-Watch people had given us safety. And remind them how you people took us.

I asked Doro to explain life on the ship. I said to describe it all in his own words. I reminded him of the food, and the cold deck of the ship, the waves splashing and the long wait that they endured.

'How can I criticise the people who saved me?' he asked. He just wanted to say how thankful he was for everything that we had done. He just kept smiling at me, saying that it was a million times better than the treatment he had in Libya. This conversation encapsulated his humility and wisdom.

I asked him to explain life on the ship with more detail. Doro just laughed, smiled and pointed at me – 'You were there, Brendan. You say it!' – and as amusing as his statement was, showing his sense of humour and his 'matter of fact' way of saying things, it was clear that Doro had already spent hours and days explaining in detail what he had been through. For Doro, the life on the ship was inconsequential in comparison to the life that he had left behind. So, maybe it's my turn to talk?

Before I describe this part of the story, it is important to recognise that the *Sea-Watch 3* is not a hotel. It simply is not designed to keep dozens of rescued people at sea for weeks on end. We do not have the medical or food supplies to sustain such a long period of time at sea. In the first hours after the rescue, we could see that the weather was still good for the rest of that day, and it would be good the following day too. We knew that we were the only ship able to respond. We decided to stay for a short while to look for other boats. We patrolled for the rest of that day, and I remember Kim introducing them to the crew, and telling them that we would stay in the area for a short while to look for others. The decision wasn't questioned at all, despite their fears and anxieties of a return to Libya. They knew that without our ship, others might drown. We sailed on.

In the night, we received news from Alarmphone that there was a report of another boat in distress. Again, this boat was in the east, and we were again in the west. It had only been a couple of days since our search for the 117 people that drowned the day before the rescue. It was agonising to feel that such a brutal event was happening again after such a short time.

This time the boat was reported to have had unconscious children on board, and that it was up to fifteen hours' sail from our location. For hours, no boats were responding to the distress calls. We tried to contact the Libyan authorities for them to go as we were so far away, and this was a boat in such desperate need of assistance, but none of their numbers worked. Hours later, a man answered the phone, but claimed not to speak English and the phone was soon dead. We continued our mission at full speed to their location. Eventually, we were told that a cargo ship was responding, and had brought the people on board. We watched on the computer tracker as they turned towards Libya, taking people back to the very hell that they had escaped from. We heard reports that the people on board were suicidal upon discovering their fate. We offered assistance, but we were just ignored. Against refugee law, this cargo ship took them back to Libya, where people just like Doro, and you, and kids just like my kids and your kids, would face the same hell that they had done everything to escape from. Meanwhile, Doro and his friends adjusted to life on the ship. Kim told them that we were continuing to search, and they all understood.

We continued our patrol for a couple of days, but we could see on the weather reports that there was a storm coming. It would not have been safe to keep the people that we had rescued at sea unnecessarily, so we sailed towards Lampedusa to ask for a safe port. We waited and were eventually denied entry. We were forced to sail north in deteriorating conditions. We passed Malta, again asking for a safe port, and again our pleas were denied. We had to sail to Sicily in the end to find shelter from storm conditions, just outside of Syracuse. Soon, we were surrounded by seven boats with blue lights on them. We were ordered into the harbour and told to anchor up. We stayed there for days, looking after the people whilst a political storm raged about our audacity at saving human lives.

The people that we'd rescued could see the land that they were dreaming of, but they weren't allowed to touch it. It was insanely cruel, but we did our best to get them through it. We played cards, music and made games together to pass the time, and mostly it worked, but these were people that had suffered terribly in Libya. Their physical scars were more than matched by their mental scars. After a few days, a tourist ship came close to us. It was packed with journalists and photographers with zoom lenses peering in on our lives. It was international news, and all of the crew were being contacted by journalists back home for interviews. I spent much of my time with the forty-seven people that we'd rescued talking about football and trying to make them feel at ease. They all knew that I supported Newcastle United as I'd talk of our previous African players and sing the songs. Some of them didn't know my name, and most didn't speak English. Often, I'd hear them calling me 'Newcastle' and sometimes as I walked by, we'd sing a football song together.

Different members of the crew all took it upon themselves to do something, anything to alleviate the underlying tension and fear that we, the crew, would succumb to political pressure and take them back to Libya. We would never do that, of course, but they were terrified, nonetheless. One day the paparazzi boat came back, and I could see that many of the rescued people were sat on floating rescue equipment and the orange fenders from the ship. They were all talking seriously about how their lives were being scrutinised by the media and they asked me what the journalists would say. I could see how their faces looked so serious, and considered how the journalists would probably write about them as if they were to be feared, showing their upset faces as 'proof' of their claims. I said, 'Who cares what they say?' and then I started singing football songs, hoping that they'd smile and stop worrying. They all just joined in, and we had such a fabulous moment together.

The next day, the photographs in the media came with headlines about how easy they were having it on the ship, how happy they looked, how healthy they looked, and all written in such a way as to prove that they were not the victims of torture as we had claimed, but instead they were economic migrants that are just here for a free ride. People back home might be convinced when they see a photograph like that with the words that they'd written, but I knew. Some of the news stories spoke about them like they were animals, but they were my friends. Matteo Salvini tweeted, threatening the crew with criminal charges. He said that we had 'facilitated illegal migration'. He said that none of the people that we had rescued would be allowed from the ship.

When the date passed that I should have flown back to be with my family, I collected my sleeping bag from my cabin and went to sleep with the rest of our guests on the rear deck. It was a small act of solidarity to show that we too are kept at sea against our will, and that their struggle is our struggle. We are one. It meant a lot to Doro when I put my sleeping bag next to his. We shared supper and played cards, and then slowly we drifted off to sleep to the sound of small waves lapping against the side of the ship, the low hum of a generator and the flip, flap of the wind against the tarpaulin awning that covered our heads.

It was about three in the morning when I was awakened by Doro kicking me in his sleep. His hands were raised above his head and he was kicking out over and over. I put my hand on his shoulder: 'Hey buddy . . . you alright?'

'Yes, Brendan, I'm fine,' he said as he woke.

'You were dreaming, buddy. Were you playing football or something?' I asked with a smile . . .

'No, Brendan, I was hanging by my hands, and they were beating me. But it was only a dream. Go back to sleep.'

Then he turned over, pulled his blankets tighter and curled into a ball. I lay there a while thinking of what he had said. A short while later, he raised his arms again in his sleep and started kicking. I didn't know whether to wake him again to tell him it's OK, or to just let him sleep through it. After a while, I thought that there is no taking away the suffering that he has endured, so just let him sleep. It broke my heart.

In the morning, he woke with a smile, just happy to be alive. 'Hey, Brendan. How are you, my brother?'

'Morning, buddy – you want some tea?' and like nothing had happened during the night, Doro started his day by stretching up out of his bed and going to check on all his friends, greeting them all with a smile. I remember feeling amazed by his inner strength. How could he keep going like that? His resilience is outstanding.

Chapter 23

The Facebook Posts

I spent some time on the ship writing about what was happening and sharing news on social media, mainly using Facebook. I thought it was important to describe and record what was really going on so that people, including friends and family would know what we were doing and why we were doing it. So much was being written in the mainstream media without any real understanding, and always from a politically biased perspective. I felt that a real witness account from somebody who was there was crucial. The next few pages are extracts taken from the Facebook posts that I wrote at the time, describing events as they happened. I share them here as a record of my own thoughts during Doro's time on the ship.

21 January 2019

Just another update. I can't get sufficient internet to post any photos, but I know many people want to know what's happening.

Reports from the people we rescued on the 19th are grim.

One guy's story is the worst that I've heard, and his scars are utterly evident. He recalled the story of each wound to me. It hurt just to listen. But I'll write about him another time.

There are very real reasons that people go to Libya, and the nature of the situation there eats them up. Several people on our ship have been auctioned off as slaves. Lots have been tortured whilst a video call is made to their families to extort money. Mothers and fathers have sold their houses to pay for the release of their sons. That is why we should never take the people back!

Despite these stories though, as our ship requests a safe port in Europe, the people on our ship are fantastic. We are trying to build a community of love on our ship. And everybody mucks in. The guy with the worst scars I've ever seen smiles and says that he is safe now, finally, after years of imprisonment, torture and abuse. He sits and washes the dishes each time we eat.

We play music together. We do fitness classes. We play cards. We talk. We pray. We sing. We have language lessons. We talk of Europe and of Africa. One Love abounds on this ship, and I am utterly privileged to be on it.

Now, tell your politicians to open the ports to some of the kindest and gentlest men that our world needs.

Finally. If you want to donate to help us continue our important work, here's the link: https://sea-watch.org/en/donate/

22 January 2019

Still waiting for a port of safety for our forty-seven guests on board the *Sea-Watch 3*.

Europe seems afraid of these gentle souls for reasons that I cannot grasp. I showed them some Go-Pro footage of their rescue today, and had to show it over and over again. They told me how afraid they were that we were the so-called Libyan Coast Guard as we bounced through the waves on the RHIB towards them. Once they heard us speak and saw my white face, they said that they knew that they were safe. They celebrated, and cried tears of relief, joy and exhaustion. The emotions are still so raw.

I've spent hours talking to them about their experiences, and I'm staggered by their humanity, by their struggle. But despite everything that they have faced, they breathe empathy with one another. They are kind and gentle to each other. They are supportive of us as a crew and feel a sense of mutual responsibility for all of us on the ship. I am awestruck by their resolve.

They've spoken of their dreams. Each one wants to work. None have spoken of Europe helping them, but of how they want to build a new life. They live in true hope. But I'm terrified for them, although I don't show it at all. For I know that once they have landed on European soil, their struggle will continue. A new chapter to their suffering will begin, with mistrust and hostility about them, because I have seen how people struggle to cope with the hostility in places like Paris, where they are forced to the streets, in the snow and the cold. May we offer them a warm heart where we can.

One boy has been telling me for days that he's fifteen years old. I looked at him, sure that he was younger. His friend told me that he is making out that he is older than he really is because he does not want to face this life as a teenager. He's tiny, and really quite adorable. He's going to own up about his real age soon. He's twelve or thirteen. I asked him what he's doing on the ship, and where he wants to go. In a second he replied, 'Marseilles'. I asked why. 'That's where my father lives,' he said. This young boy is crossing the deadliest border on the planet to meet his dad. And he's doing it alone! Open the ports, man!

23 January 2019

My friend Doro and I have been talking a lot. I said that I'm ashamed that the doors to Europe are closed to people like him. People who have suffered. People whose lives are at risk. He said, 'Don't blame them. Some people, they only see skin.'

Doro is incredibly intelligent. He speaks seven languages, but it's not just that. He is wise. I mean, really wise. I gravitate to him constantly. He explained the situation in Libya vividly. He wants the world to know what is happening and what they did to him. My gentle friend, who is wise, kind, and courageous has experienced what nobody should. He inspires me in every conversation. I wish I could take him to England, but, you see, some people, they only see skin!

26 January 2019

You show me a fighting aged male and I will show you a man who can work. Show me the man that you're frightened of, and I will show you a gentle soul who is scared. You show me an economic migrant, an invader, or a crook, and I will show you a mirror. For we are all the sons and daughters of migrants. We, as people, have always moved. And we have all benefited from their misery.

In order for you to be rich, to buy cheap clothes and to talk on your phone, someone will slave for you. It is our ease of living that has made them poor. It is our exploitation that makes them run. Not just the West, but the rich all over. We are the creators of migration, the benefactors and the blind. We turn our eyes from their suffering yet expect them to take all that comes. We buy brands that exploit, and expect everything for cheap, cheap, cheap.

But when a boy or a man cannot see how they can survive, we expect them to drown silently in their poverty, whilst we book our holidays in the sun. And we will use our passports to fly to almost any destination on this earth. We, the rich can seek employment wherever we like, and we can just pop to Paris for a weekend away. But when the man who suffers for our opulence wants to do the same, we say no, don't come, you should stay.

We, the creators of their misery, define ourselves as the victims of their pain. We cry and complain that someone steals the job that we're too lazy to do. We take their oil, their minerals, their produce and their lives, yet it is 'we' who call 'them' the crooks. And it is we that call ourselves the victims of their pain. You say that they come for our welfare state, yet I've met thousands of people crossing this sea, and every single one of them wanted to work. Can you say that about the people back home? I certainly can't!

You talk of losing our culture but when we can turn our backs to the poor, then I think it's a culture that we can lose. You say that we should help our homeless first, yet when we see the man on the streets, we walk by. We each live in a blanket of self-righteousness, myself included, stating that others should do something to change. Be it for the homeless, the lonely or the displaced, we form our opinions from the warmth and comfort of our homes.

But unless you have walked one mile in their shoes, then don't tell them where they should go. Because we are their reflection. We were all made the same. It is by chance that we were born with opportunity, as it is by chance that they were born in the dust. And it could be by chance that our choices are taken away. Their struggle is our struggle, for if it was not them, it would be us.

You think that leaving all that you have known is easy? You think that crossing that sea is a choice? Then you don't know how many are lost to this journey. You don't know the pain that they take. And if you want to talk about choices, then you should acknowledge that it is only us who can choose!

We have one life. Let's not waste it on hate. Only love!

29 January 2019

Some people are asking why I'm doing this, so here goes:

I believe in a world where compassion is king. Where cruelty is rejected. Where it doesn't matter where a person comes from, whether they're old or young, whether they're black or white, what their sexuality is, or whether they're male, female, or anything else that is used to define, divide, or separate.

I believe in one human race where we are all equal. And I believe that these beliefs are worth standing up for. In the face of adversity. In spite of hate. When it's hard to do. Even when it affects you and those that you love. Some things are worth the stand!

I want to live in a world where kindness is commonplace. Where we work together to help each other through. Where if we see someone suffering, we hold out a helping hand. It's not easy, but if we want that world, then we have to make it happen. We have to live by our beliefs.

If we don't live by what we believe in, then what we believe in will not live. That's how I see it anyway. So, when I know that people are escaping from hell, and that they're being drowned in our sea in order to create a deterrent for others who would come, then I feel compelled to do something about it.

Empathy is not easy without ears that listen. And if we listen to why people want to escape from Libya then it should be easy to understand that it is wrong to turn away from their suffering.

We are being criminalised. We are, all of the crew, being accused of 'facilitating illegal migration', yet all we did was rescue people who otherwise would have drowned.

How, in anyone's universe, is saving lives at sea a crime? #openheartsandopenports

31 January 2019

Today we said goodbye to our forty-seven friends. We've lived side by side since the 19th of January after the rescue. I'm heartbroken and overjoyed. I'm filled with hope and fear.

Heartbroken to say goodbye to my friends. Overjoyed that they are finally safely in Europe. Filled with a new hope through witnessing the most incredible solidarity that I could have imagined. And terrified of how others in Europe will treat them.

I have been to Lesvos, Paris, Calais, and Dunkirk. I've seen with my own eyes the suffering and squalor that is so horribly commonplace in Europe today. And I've seen the comments and heard the whispers of hate. That's what frightens me. How will they be treated now that they have left the ship.

Also, I am proud! I am proud to have been amongst the first to welcome them. To show them kindness and compassion. I'm proud that we were the ones that they shared their stories with for the first time. I'm proud that we were the first to give them comfort and hope.

I'm proud of all of my shipmates too. We've all worked so

Doro

hard. I'll share stories of the last few weeks in due course. But for now, I look forward to returning to my family, and seeing all my friends that have shared such solidarity.

Without your voice this would not have changed. I share your scream to the world to change.

One love!

Chapter 24

Disembarkation

And that was it. Eventually, after days of keeping our friends at sea, some European countries agreed it was time to take the people that had been rescued, and that we should sail to Catania in Sicily, and disembark Doro and his friends, for them to start a new life. We told them it was over. I'll never forget it. The overwhelming sense of relief was tangible and so incredibly personal but deeply interconnected with one another and with us as a team. First there was a lot of jumping up and down, clapping and excitement. Some people just dropped to their knees and sobbed with a mixture of joy, relief and sheer emotion as the tension slipped away. Soon, this part of their journey would be all over, but what a moment, for each of those forty-seven people had endured their own personal hell, and that was the moment that they knew it was over.

It turned out the Italian authorities had reached a deal with other European countries, so that if we were allowed to bring the people into their safe port, then the people that we had rescued would be transferred to other countries. Italy didn't want to take responsibility for looking after all of our friends and felt that the rest of Europe should shoulder some of the responsibility for all of the people arriving on their shores. It's a fair point. Why should these arrival countries have to take on these responsibilities alone? I believe that there should be a distribution deal between the different EU states, and an agreement of responsibility sharing. However, the fact that there is not an agreement between our politicians is not the fault of the vulnerable people who are escaping Libya in these flimsy boats, and they should not be detained at sea while our politicians squabble. I found it to be one of the greatest injustices that I had experienced – to be treated like a criminal – but to our rescued friends it was just another injustice, the salt in their wounds.

As we approached the port of Catania, we were saying our last goodbyes. Doro and I spent some time together. I promised to keep in touch with him and we spoke about the experience, but mainly it was silence between me and him. Neither of us wanted to break.

At one point, Kim came to say his goodbyes to them, and he was instantly picked up and carried on shoulders by those whose rescue he had coordinated. One by one we met and said our goodbyes. I remember vividly the young boy, maybe fifteen years old, who came to say goodbye. This brave boy who said he was fifteen years of age, but looked so much younger, had made a paper model of the rescue to give to me as a thank you. A paper boat coloured with crayons which I shall treasure for ever. He spoke no English, and my French is minimal. He struggled with my name, so called me 'Newcastle' as most of my conversations with the young boys were about football. He came to me so quietly, trying not to cry. He simply said, 'Hey, Newcastle. You. Here. For ever', and he pointed to his heart. I hugged him with my face over his shoulder so that he couldn't see the tears in my eyes.

We got closer and could see the reception committee waiting for us. There was quite a crowd in the harbour. Journalists, medics, police, immigration officials and politicians all looked on stone-faced. Some were wearing surgical masks as if they were somehow frightened of catching a disease that they'd contained with us at sea for two weeks. There was little joy waiting for our friends out there. It was quite intimidating. Officials came on board. One border guard at the back wasn't wearing a surgical mask, and was just smiling, trying to show humanity. The woman at the front was as serious as could be. I put out my hand and said welcome on board, knowing that she'd refuse it. She just looked me in the eye and shook her head. I smiled back at her as warmly as I could, but nothing would defrost her reaction. Others showed kindness, smiled, and waved to us from the dock. That contrast of welcomes was so stark, with some convinced that we had just brought in a boatload of trouble, but others recognising that there were human beings on our ship.

After a short while, we were told that they would take the children first and then the men, so they all lined up ready to go. As Issa, the first to go, was told he could leave, he hugged each of the rescue team as he walked towards the gangplank. He stopped halfway across it and turned, making a heart shape with his hands. One by one they left, and we clapped them as they walked away to their new lives. First the children, and then the men.

Doro waited to be one of the last to leave, but he couldn't really speak. Words were not necessary.

When it was his turn to go, he came with a piece of paper with a handwritten note of thanks which I shall always keep.

Doro

He just put it in my hand. He was biting his bottom lip; he couldn't look me in the eye. He simply nodded, and then a quick hug, and off he went as sombrely as I've ever seen him. This was the moment that he'd suffered so much to achieve, and all he could think of were his friends, the crew of the *Sea-Watch 3* that he was leaving behind.

Chapter 25

Italy

When I was in the ship, I think Europe is with me, you know? Because we was having everything. We was having freedom from Libya. We was having better food than in Libya. We was having a place to sleep more than Libya prison and more than in those Libya homes. When Kim came and said that Italy would let the ship come in, that time I don't feel like to come down, because that time I feel like I am in my home, in the ship. When Kim come to talk to us, I look at Kim and I look at the team and I think how we lived together, and I started to cry. I see you too, Brendan, and you are crying. It was big emotion. I want to stay together with you people for ever, but that can't be.

When the ship was moving. When we was going to Catania, I was very happy because before I didn't believe we will come down, because a lot of people go back.* There was one ship who go up to international and they return them back to Libya. We was thinking about that, but you

---

* When Doro says 'come down', he means 'arrive in Europe'.

people make us to see that one day we will come down. So when we was going to Catania, I was happy. But the time that they came to tell us it is time to come down, I was having big emotions. I was thinking I don't want to come down to leave you people.

That very day, I was very sad. The thing make me cry, even. I was thinking, 'Which day am I going to see good people like you people? You people saved our life, you know?' That thing made me cry and I was thinking a lot of you people, because we people, we stay together for over two weeks. Everybody was good to each other, you know? And you people learn us plenty things about life. We was blind, the time we come from Libya, we was blind. We didn't know the world; it has plenty things inside the world. You people learn us plenty thing. So for me, the thing that makes me cry is: which day are we going to see you people again? I don't know how to explain it. Is it God will make me that I will see in my life other people good like you people? That whole thing I was thinking about. Then I was saying also, 'Even if we say to you people "Thank You", it is not enough. What are we going to do for you people to be happy more?' So that thing made me sad. When I was coming down from the ship, I didn't even want to come down.

I write on paper. Me and Ismail, we write on paper for all of you people, you know? And the moment we live in the ship, we will know each other small, not too much. So that time I give you that paper, it is something in my heart. I write it from my heart. The time we went to leave the ship I feared to look all of you people in your eyes. I was getting big emotion, so I cannot look you people in the eye. I don't know how to explain that. It was emotion. I was feeling very, very, very sad. I was thinking, 'Which day are we going to stay together again? Like we was in the ship, we was family, you know? We was like brothers. Eating together, cooking together.' Because I see those experience. I was living with Arab people. When they cook their food, they will cook their own food. It will be different, what they eat and what we eat. But for you people, everybody will eat one food, sleep in one place, you know? That thing is something like, I am living with my blood people, like my mom, my father, and my real family, you know? I feel like that. That's why when we was leaving each other, I cannot look you people in the eye.

So we went in a line to leave the ship and me, I go to the back of the line. Me and Ismail, we were the last persons to leave the ship. And Ibrahim. So we were thinking, Which day are we going to see you people. I feel emotion, you know? The time I was coming down from the ship, every step I was thinking to go back, you know? Every step I was thinking to go back. That's why when I go back through and the people see us and check us, I just go straight. I go sit on the bus and sit down. I was crying. And everybody, my friends, are saying, 'Don't cry, you will see them again.' Up to the camp. The only thing I was thinking is that I was saying to you people, goodbye for ever. That's why I was crying.

In that time, I didn't even see Italian people. Me in my own imagination, me, I was not thinking about Italy. I was thinking to stay in the boat with you people. That time, me I, up to we go in the camp, I didn't think of it as I was in Italy, you know? I was thinking about Sea-Watch. Because we are having peace. We are having everything like we are living in Europe. Then they searched us and also they give us food, and also they give us one plastic bag which had clothes and shoes. After, when we go up to the camp, they carry me and Amin and Bubacar, they carry us three to help the doctors to check people and to site them in the camp. Me, I was one of those three people helping the Italian people in the camp.

After, inside the camp, the first day, they introduced people. About seven countries come. There is one person there and he is from Senegal, but he didn't speak all the languages, so after, they call me to help them interpret to all the people. The camp is not like those camps in Libya. It is a European Union camp. So the camp is like a hotel for us to be truthful. It is a good place. Everybody had him own bed and a toilet. It is a new camp. So they say it is created by the European Union. So it was good. The food used to come every morning, in the afternoon and in the night. It was spaghetti, and sometimes chicken.

After one day, they come and introduce people, Italian police. They said that it is me who bring the boat. After we had been there three weeks, France takes seven people. Me I was part of those seven people, but they didn't take me, so me I stay in Italy for over a month. Some go France, some go Germany, Portugal, Romania, Lithuania and Luxembourg. They said I will not go to France because they tell me that I should go to the court. They said those bambinos, those small boys on the ship, they said they will give them paper in Italy if they say who bring the boat, so those small people, they said it is me that bring the boat.

After, they carry me to the court. The first day I said I don't hear any language. I only hear my language. No French, no English, no nothing. I only hear my own language. After, they drop me back, because they don't have any interpreter that can hear my language, because in Africa they only speak my language in my country and in Mali. Those two countries have my language. So they don't have any interpreter, so they bring me back to the camp. So I stay one week and after, they carry me back to the court. They said they have interpreter and I see this time that there are two lawyers from France. So after they talk to me, I didn't talk. The judge they talk, my lawyers, they talk. That was the second time we go. After then they take me back. So the lawyers say to me to say my name, I say my name. I say no problem. They said, OK sit down, don't talk.

I can understand why Doro said that he didn't hear any language. It must have been so intimidating for Doro, a man who grew up on a fishing boat and a goat herding farm, to be expected to stand testimony in a court where he is speaking his second language, where he knows that any mistake in his articulation of events could lead to imprisonment or deportation. Despite his ability to make himself understood in several languages, legal parlance is often difficult for native speakers, let alone those who have picked up languages in the way Doro has. On his first court appearance he had no legal representation, which is so commonplace for asylum seekers in the UK and in Europe today. Decisions are made without real understanding of circumstances. Who could blame Doro for insisting on an interpreter who could explain in his own first language?

I don't know those lawyers before. I don't even know they are from France. I don't know nothing about lawyers. I don't know nothing about justice. Me, I was just following police people. They will carry me, I will go to the court.

They will bring me back. After, they said I will go France. This case finished. I win the case. They talk to the man who used to interpret. It is him who tell me that. He said, 'Your case is finished. Tomorrow you are going to France.' I was feeling happy because my friends, they go. Ismail and Ibrahim too, we are long-time friends, since in Libya. We know each other since in the prison. It's not easy. So I feel like to be with them, so I was very happy.

So in the morning, after I get up, I see two people who come. Those two people I see before in the courthouse. After then, they tell me they are my lawyers. They said they will take me to the airport with this woman and then I will go France. After, he tell me, 'You don't have any problem now. Even if you stay in Italy, Italy should give you papers.' Those lawyers tell me that, but they say they will carry me to France. After they carry me to the airport, I enter the plane from Sicily with the woman up to Rome. The woman carry me the airport. She drop me there and she give my contact in France to somebody in Paris. So only me from Rome to Paris on the plane. It was my second time on a plane. In Angola, I have been on a plane. I never been on those kind of planes, you know. There is plenty people. Everybody was sitting. It was very organised.

All this time, I was on the phone to Doro almost every day. I had flown back to England and just went back to work. I was a few days later than expected, but fortunately my employers were supportive. Everyone I knew had seen what had happened on the news and were telling me how worried they were for me, but all that time I was only worried for Doro and all the other people that we'd rescued. I knew that one ordeal was over, but for some a new nightmare would begin. Some of the forty-seven people that we'd helped were immediately taken to countries like Portugal and France. I knew they'd be alright. Others headed for Estonia and Romania, and I was unable to tell them anything about what their new lives would be like, for I'd never been to those places. I knew that some of them would have their asylum applications rejected, and that some would be allowed to stay. I knew that some would be welcomed with warmth, but others with hostility. I was happy that each one of them had escaped Libya, but was rightfully concerned about their new lives.

When Doro told me that he was going to court, I was terrified for him. Would a rejection break him? I reassured him as best I could, but I could sense how nervous he was. The other six people that France had agreed to take had already left, and Doro was just waiting for his day in court. On the phone he spoke softly and slowly. He was so solemn. I could tell he was scared. Then one day, the phone rang. It was Doro: 'Brendan! It's over!' The next day he was due to fly to Paris and make his asylum claim in France. It was like music to my ears. Still, I was anxious. Would they grant him asylum? Would he be returned to The Gambia?

Chapter 26

France

When I come to Paris, after, the woman come with my pictures, asking people if they have seen me. She say, 'Is this you?'

I say, 'Yes.'

She carried me to the train station. There was no metro. It was night. After, we sleep in the hotel. In the morning I entered into the metro and it took me directly to Bourges. On the train, it was amazing. I was looking everywhere. I was thinking of the journey I make to come here. I was thinking, No, is it a dream? No, I'm not in France. I looked. It was beautiful. It was nice. It was freedom. And it looked beautiful. It was humanity. And everywhere I go, people used to talk to me. They used to welcome me. I didn't know them. They didn't know me. It is a humanitarian life here in Europe. Everybody respect everyone.

The woman give me to one other woman who take me to the place. They give me one room, so I was there. After, I asked for my friends. They say they are not there. They not in the same place. They are in Vierzon, but me, I was in Bourges. I was not happy. I was talking bullshit. I was displaying. I say I want to be with my friends. After, the woman said, just take your time. Just see how it is and stay here for a small time. After small time you will see your friends. They will give you paper. You will have your own house, and you will go see your friends any time you feel like. After I understand the situation, I calmed down.

Doro was suffering as a result of his experiences over the last few years. He had grown used to incarceration, and the dehumanisation that he faced on a daily basis must have left him feeling as though he was in a constant fight for his rights. These are experiences and feelings that don't fade so easily. He must have felt as though the whole world was against him, and much of it was. To be separated from the others was distressing for Doro. He had built up respect from them over years on the move, so to see the others that were sent to France being in one place together, and knowing that almost all of the others that we rescued were still together in Italy, all combined to compound Doro's feelings of isolation. It was as though his arrival in this 'promised land' was a broken fantasy and that all of his suffering was for nought. Here he was, separated from his friends in a strange, cold place, where he knew nobody and felt like nobody. Explaining to Doro that he had to bide his time, and that things would be better in time, was no easy task.

Me, I have luck. Because the first food that I have in my new place in France, I cook for myself. They give me money; I go up to the shop go and buy things. I go and buy food and I put it in the fridge. So I cook my African food. I was happy. So happy. I cook rice and chicken. It was sweet. The first night in France, I call my friends in Libya and everywhere and tell them I am in France, and nobody believe me. Some of them are telling me you came out from hell and go to paradise, because Libya is hell.

The first time that I call them and said hello to my mom, wife, children, I am in Europe, and I am in France, they all cry. I now asked my mom, 'Why are you crying, you should be happy.'

She said, 'I am crying but this cry is a happiness cry because I never believed in this day. And today I hear the sound of my son and him tell me I am in Europe. It is unimaginable.'

And my wife, she said, 'Every day when I get up and I go to the market, I hear people ask, saying you should find somebody else to marry because your husband is already died. Better than to sit down here and to wait for him. You will be old here. Nobody will marry you. And nobody will look after you. And today I am happy that you called, and you are alive.'

In the apartment, we was three people. We was sharing everything together. A few months later, they carry me to another place, and they give me my apartment. I was happy because I didn't believe I will come in France, you know? After some time, I was not staying with my friends. I was not happy. I was stressed. After, you explain to me. You talked to me, and I understand. Because I think before, when I come in France, I will go and stay with Ismail, with Ibrahim, with all of them, you understand? It's what they tell me on the plane. They said you will go and join your friends. So I come and I didn't meet any-body. I was stressed. I was telling them it was better for me to go back to Italy. Because it was hard for me to

understand. I was lonely. I was staying alone. I was thinking about what I had passed in Libya, those hard things,
because I was alone, and I don't know nobody. And the
people I know, they were far from me.

It was that time that you sent me Catherine. She said to
me, 'Don't worry. You will just spend small time here. One
day they will give you papers, and after then you go and
join your friends any time you feel like, you will see your
friends.' And you too, Brendan. You too advise me. You
forget!

I hadn't forgotten. At the time, Doro was lonely and scared. He
had been left without any of his friends who had been on our
ship. He knew that all of the others who had been taken in by
France were all staying together in a shared flat, but Doro was
in a flat without anyone that he knew, and he really needed
support which at first, he wasn't getting.

After experiencing so much horror, Doro was alone for
much of his time with only his thoughts for company. Over the
phone, I could hear how his mood was changing as the days
passed. The memories of what had happened to him, the lone-
liness, and the fear of being rejected and sent back, were
tangible. I spoke to him as much as I could and remember him
wanting to go back to Italy where some of his friends were,
and to spend time with Bubacar. I reassured him that he would
make friends in France, and that eventually Bubacar and the
others will be taken from Italy. I explained how his future as a
French-speaking man would probably be better in France
than just returning to the unknown.

After a while, I managed to find a friend of a friend who helps
refugees and asylum seekers in Bourges. Catherine went to
meet him and immediately helped get him the psychological

support that he needed. There are lots of people like Catherine in France, in England, Italy and Greece. In fact, all over the world, there are people who witness suffering and feel that they should do something about it. In England, we have a marvellous charity called 'Refugees at Home' which helps house asylum seekers with people who live here. It helps give them a start, form a support network. The same kind of thing happens throughout France, and Catherine is one such volunteer.

When we were in Bourges together, Doro took me to Catherine's home, where she lived with her family. Also staying with her was a young man from Afghanistan who spoke excellent English and was learning to speak French. I'd found Catherine through an online refugee volunteers' group. When it became clear that Doro was struggling to maintain his mental well-being, I wrote a note in the volunteer support group asking for help. A wonderful woman called Christine suggested Catherine and said that she lived nearby. Catherine is a rock for people like Doro. When she met him, she immediately sought psychiatric help as Doro was reliving his moments of torture over and over in his mind. She helped him to get the medical help for his physical injuries too. She took him to meet other asylum seekers, and Doro was slowly able to build friendships in his new life. Volunteers like Catherine, supporting refugees in their local communities, are real life savers. I cannot overstate the important role that these volunteers make.

After I calm down, I started to write my story. Every day when I am sitting alone, I started to write. After I tell you, I say I am writing my story. Because every time I was sitting alone, I was thinking about my past. It was hard. You should have somebody to share with. You should have somebody to talk to. You know? Not be alone. That time I think I will go mad.

And then they started to explain us the life over here. I started to go outside. And then Catherine started to carry me places. She is a good woman. She is a good woman like you. You two do a lot for me. God will bless you. It is because of you that I am happy today. You are part of my life now. And God bless all of your family. Because after when Catherine saw me, and Catherine know my situation she said yes, this man suffering. She started to carry me places. She started to talk to me. She started to carry me to the library and plenty places. So I started to be happy. And every day when I am alone, you used to call me every day. God bless your life. You didn't give up.

The day they bring my papers, they bring the envelope, I open it and my friend said, 'You should be happy. You stay here one month, and they give you papers.' And they give me papers to stay here, you know? For ten years! Yes, me too, I started to be happy. I called Catherine in the morning, and she come and carry me to one place where people used to talk about their story. They used to help you and change your mind and learn French also. So life started to change for me. I am a refugee. I have permission to stay.

Doro had video-called me too. I couldn't believe it at the time. I thought that there must have been a mistake because I know the asylum applications usually take months and even years to be heard. I was concerned that such a prolonged wait would see Doro suffer in the same way that I'd seen others suffering from the seemingly endless waiting game that refugees have to endure, with uncertainty, without being able to live and build for the future, and with fears of rejection and deportation. I saw his excited face beaming from ear to ear. I tried to remain calm and told him that I was happy for him. For sure, he may have received some sort of paperwork, but I couldn't believe that he'd been accepted so quickly. I checked and double checked. He showed me the papers over the phone. My heart leaped across my chest. I was screaming with relief. Tears filled my eyes, and that was it, we were both looking at each other over our phones with smiles and tears of joy.

All seven of the people that had been taken to France after we had left them in Syracuse were accepted as refugees in France. Some were given papers that would allow them to stay for five years, after which they would have to reapply, but Doro was given ten years. He will be able to apply for French citizenship. I don't know what happened to all of the forty-seven people that we had rescued. Some were sent to Romania, where Bubacar has since received refugee status and is now working and starting his new life. Others have had their initial claims rejected, mainly those who were taken to Romania and Estonia. Some are still waiting for their applications to be processed. Others have been rejected and are now appealing their decisions. Some of those are now on the run, heading to cities like Paris, where thousands of this diaspora are sleeping rough on the streets. The Sudanese man that I spoke of earlier, who scored the most incredible goal in our ship's football match, has made it to the UK, and is now waiting for his asylum application to be heard.

I know that at least three of the people that we had rescued have since been deported back to their home countries. I am glad that at least they are not in Libya, and am proud to have played my part in saving them from the sea. I look back to that moment on their boat, when they realised that our rescue RHIB was not the Libyan Coast Guard, ready to take them back to hell. I remember how they celebrated their freedom and their safety. It hurts to think that some of them have been sent away, and that some of them are possibly on the cold streets of Paris tonight, but I know that my part in that was simply trying to stop them from drowning, and none of them drowned. Everything else is beyond my control.

When I come in France, I come in France in March. Five months later, when they give me papers, my everything come OK. They do me operation for my eye. The first time I go to the hospital, when they check my eye, they say it is because of the cataract. The white cataract is in my eye. That's why my eye is not seeing anything. So after saying that, they give me medical thing. I used to take the drugs and put some medicine in my eye. So afterwards they do the operation and come out the cataracts. When they come out, the cataracts, my eye still blind, it's not seeing nothing. They give me again two months. They say my eye will see again in two months' time. In two months' time also my eye didn't see nothing. I returned back to my doctor. They say they check everything, but they think it's dead bloods inside my eye. When I go back there, and my eye is not seeing anything. And my eye is not the same, because my eye is not in the middle. My eye will stay like this.

After they do operation for my eye, they do operation for my stomach in the same hospital. The operation for the stomach was in December 2019. And I was in the hospital for two weeks and I come out and the doctor give me one month to go back to the appointment. After, when I

go back to the appointment, they come out all the nylons.*
After he tell me it's OK. They give me medicines and I
used to take the medicines. So they check everything and
they say it's alright. Me myself, I feel it's OK, it's alright,
thank God. The stomach is good because before, when I
was eating, it used to pain me and used to come big. When
we were on the ship, I used to tell you that my stomach
was pain me, and I used to shit blood before. But now it
has all stopped. It is all OK. They do good operation.
Now I feel OK. Before when I work, my stomach used to
pain me, but now I can work throughout the day no problem. Thank God for the stomach.

From when I have my papers, I tell Catherine I want to
do something. So they take me one place and they find me
information to learn and I go to school. I was learning
French and I was learning what I should do in the future.
I say I want to be an electrician. So I was learning in
French. And after, in the evening I was learning electric. It
is that what I want to be in the future. I want to be an
electrician.

I stay in school for six months, but then I sign contract
to work in a farm. I do salad, lettuce, carrots, plenty
things. Because I do that before. I do that in Libya and in
my village. It is a big association, and it helps people who
come here and get papers. Later I went back to school to
be an electrician.

In my new life in France, I am happy for Sea-Watch and
you. It is because of you people that we go up to this level,
that we go up to this step. My grandfather used to tell me,
'Anything you put in your farm, it is that you will record in

* Take out the stitches.

the end of your days.' If you people didn't give us hope, we would not be here today. Brendan, let's tell the truth. When I am chatting with people it is the topic we used to talk. You people never discourage us. You always give advice.

Since this interview, Doro has passed his electrician course at college and is now working as an electrician. We still speak and message each other every week and Doro is starting to make a living for himself. He still struggles to adjust to his new life, which is very different to where he came from. He misses his family every day and dreams of being reunited with them one day.

Chapter 27

The Future

I have regret because I don't see my family for many years now. I have regret for that. But I am in Europe now. I have life. The wounds I have and the treatment I have, if I go back in Libya, I don't think that life is safe. I have four operations now and I think I have hope to make it. I have hope, but the only thing that make me lose hope is helping my family and wanting to be with my family.

Some people are saying here that I can try for paper for my family to come to France. Some people are saying that I cannot go to see them because of the paper they give me. Sometimes I think I should work here until the remainder of my life. I should work here until I die. But for me, I just want to see my family.

Right now, what I want to do is to go in my country and build a house for my family. Have my business and small work. I have land. My grandfather leave me land. In Africa you can make it if you have a foundation. I am looking for a foundation. I don't want to be here until I die. My mom is old. She pay rent and my sons they are growing, and they will not see their father. And they will not have any responsibility, any education. All that, it eat me in the night. I didn't sleep sometimes. This is why I am looking for a job and maybe in two or three years' time I have good foundation and I will go back.

The first thing I regret in my life is my mom sell the house to give me freedom. The second, somebody's daughter is waiting for five long years and waiting for me. They didn't know whether I am alive or dead. The third is for my children. The youngest one has never seen me. He just hear me on the phone and see my pictures. Is it one day that I will manage to repair all of those faults, oh my God. Is it one day that I will sit down and repair what I have done in my life, oh my God. Is it one day that I will be able to make people happy without suffering some wickedness?

Since Doro left The Gambia, the long-time dictator Yahya Jammeh has been removed from power, but many problems still remain. Thousands of displaced people have returned to a country where a fragile government is struggling to make any real progress after decades of Jammeh's rule. Gambians from all over Europe have been deported back to The Gambia, some having already built new lives in Europe. Neighbouring countries, like Senegal, have taken a greater share of the people who left, with some people never wanting to leave and some wanting to be able to return home. It's a complicated issue.

And one day I want to create an association. The association for help of immigrants in the country of Maghreb. In the countries of Libya, Algeria, Tunisia, and Morocco, if I get the power. I know I am 100 per cent sure that I cannot change the wickedness of some of the people of Maghreb, but I can give experience so people will not fall inside that wickedness. For me, when I get support, nobody will enter into Libya. I get the way to stop people and I know the way. And nobody should enter the slavery. Still now there is slavery in Libya, and everybody knows it. They deny it, and they do not stop it. When a hundred people wake up in Libya, fifty people will not return home with peace, they will dump someone and take their money. They will kill them. They will take them and make them work and not pay them. Full day work. Some people they will carry them and bring them to a house and lock them up and sell them to other people. And some people they will carry the blacks and force them to fuck them, to fuck them in the back. We see that in the prison. You cannot do nothing. They will take them, mainly Nigerian men, and he will fuck them every day.

But when you show them that you want to die, they will not do that. They fear that. With all their wickedness, when you show them you do not care about life, they will take you small, small. But when you show them that you fear guns or wounds or something like that, they have power. I showed them that I have wounds, I am not afraid of everything, and they fear that. You want to show me I will die and then we will all die. I am not afraid.

If you know how to speak their language, they will fear you, because they think that you will be dealing with their big men. When I was in Libya, they don't want any blacks. Any foreigner, they will exploit like a slave, beating you, like in the time of our grandfathers in the slavery. And without no sympathy or pity. And after, they will not give you good food. If you want to complain they will shoot you and kill you. Everybody gets a gun. Even children. But blacks are always the slave.

Why are we making this journey? Why do we decide to suffer for nothing? I want to give advice for everyone. I said everybody is welcome in the land of Adam and Eve. Everybody comes to find a good thing, not a bad thing. Then they experience a suffering. In the end of the story, I realised I regret why I came in this land.

These days and in the last days and I was thinking about my grandfather. My name is Mo Doro Ҫoumãñẹh. And the name of Mo, they give me in Libya because in the end of my last ending in Libya, it was 2018 and 2019, I come stand like a helper. I know how to speak Arab. I know everything about the deal of Libya. And I know good people and bad people. Any time a person fell into a problem, I used to explain to them I go carry you. Even people they go to prison, I go find soldiers, who are friends with me, and I pay them small money and they go take people from the prison. I help people in Libya since I was there up to fifty people in the prison. And where I create a small mosque where we could pray every day in Bangala house. And we come to be respected by the Arab people because they believe in Allah. And I created small mosque for fifty people who used to pray every day until Ramadan finished. And every day the Arab people give us what we want. They give us respect. No police, no mafia. The man in the house is so grateful. He put two shops inside the house. And in the shops, he gets what he wants. And everybody in every room is paying him. The house name is Bangala house in Zuwara.

Fifty people in the rooms all invited by me. Some of them I carried them from the prison. Some of them from the streets. Some of them go work and run from slavery and they meet me and explain to me their problem. I leave them in that house. Some of them they get themselves. They get work and get their own houses. Everybody got somewhere to go. Some went to Tunisia. Some went to Algeria. Some crossed into Europe.

Today, I thank God. Plenty people are calling me and saying that I am welcome in Europe and why God gave me the peace. And they call me Mo. Why they give me the name Mo? It is helper. And we know your heart is clean to help people and everywhere you go people will help you. I thank God.

Every survivor of this journey has a different experience. Some have escaped from the most monstrous regimes in the world. Some people have faced cruelty at home in different ways to Doro's experience. Some have fled war and famine. Others have left due to extreme poverty. People in the West cast easy suspicions that every one of the people on these boats is an economic migrant. They have no idea what they're escaping and take no time to understand the complexity of the situation as a whole. Others insist that every one of them is a refugee, and while it is entirely true that nearly every single one of them has escaped a nightmare in Libya, it is important to recognise that not all of them have left home due to war, famine and persecution. The truth often lies somewhere between these perspectives. Whatever your thoughts on their motives for coming to Europe, nobody deserves the treatment that so many of them receive in Libya, and nobody deserves to drown in the sea. To return them to a country from which they have escaped is monstrous and we should resist that at every turn.

People talk of economic migrants as though making a decision to leave home is easy. Like walking away from all that you
have known, your culture and traditions, your friends and
families, is just a choice to go and earn a little extra money. It
is strange that nobody has a problem with someone travelling
from Dublin to London for a new job, or from Arizona to Se-
attle. Or even leaving from New York to Rome for work isn't
seen as an issue, despite the fact people are crossing conti-
nents, and even travelling further. Some people in the UK felt
resentment towards economic migrants coming from Middle
and Eastern Europe and that was certainly part of the reason
that many people voted for Brexit. Today, as before the referendum, there is still greater anger shown towards migrants
who come from the Middle East and Africa, with blame being
apportioned to them for every social problem that you can
imagine. Yet each and every one of those that I have met
wanted to work. They really don't want hand-outs. Nobody just
chooses to be a refugee. Many of those making dangerous
crossings of the Mediterranean or the English Channel have
paid thousands to the smugglers. Some of them have absolutely nothing when they arrive on our shores. Others have
money, but in my experience they pretty much all want to
work and pay taxes. We have to ask what really drives the
internal mental conflicts that some people have in relation to
immigration. What is at the heart of our willingness to either
return people like Doro to hell or to allow them to drown in the
sea? In many cases this is just racism. Only a fool couldn't
recognise that.

Our Western European perspectives ignore our still exist-
ing empires. The colonies are still there. They're unofficial and
unrecognised. We simply outsource our imperialism to corpor-
ations that exploit the people for their labour and export their

resources and wealth. We are an empire by proxy. As a recent poster campaign by Greg Bunbury, founder of Black Outdoor Art, pointed out: 'We did not come to Britain. Britain came to us.' The far-right parties see immigration as an invasion and call the survivors of this perilous journey 'fighting-aged males'. But I know them as just humans like me and you. Normal people. Why not call them working-aged males? Because it doesn't fit the narrative. We wouldn't get frightened if politicians were to call them workers. I know people who have fled war, and I know people like Doro, who, after a journey he hadn't intended to make, that almost killed him, and from which he could not possibly return, found his way to the sea. Who are we, any one of us, to tell him what to do, and where he can and can't go? None of us have ever earned that right.

Chapter 28

Hopes and Dreams

Since I interviewed Doro in Bourges, I have returned to my family in England. I am blessed by the fortunate life that I have, and to have met people like Doro and encountered their perspectives on life. Each of my daily troubles is reduced and I feel truly lucky never to have lived through their experiences. I recognise that so much of my opportunity is just through the luck of where I was born. I don't feel the need to constantly run the rat race, but to enjoy moments in life a little more. I still work in the Fire Service, enjoying the camaraderie of my team, attending incidents, and helping my community. It's a job I love and feel pride for. I live at home with my girlfriend, and my son. Tragically, in June 2022, my daughter Jennifer died in a car crash. My feeling of loss is endless, and I feel like I have earned a cloud that will follow me for ever, wherever I go. Jennifer loved Doro and I know that she would have wanted me to continue in my efforts to help refugees and to continue to support people like Doro wherever I can.

I have continued my efforts to help refugees, both at home

and at sea, returning from another mission in April 2022 where we rescued 211 people. Sadly seventeen people drowned right in front of us, and another boat sank that we just didn't get to. It is estimated that ninety-six people drowned on that boat. Europe shoulders much of the blame for their deaths and it is an injustice that I intend to strive to change for as long as I am capable and for as long as there is still a need.

In 2014, around the time that Doro was leaving The Gambia, having seen his fishing business taken by the government and his friend imprisoned, I was in Afghanistan, serving with the British Army. I would probably have been one of those people who said that they want to help 'real refugees', but not these 'economic migrants'. I might not have put it quite like that, but certainly I would have thought that the difference between one and the other was important and easy to make. I had read in the news about boats capsizing in the Central Mediterranean Sea, particularly the shipwrecks of April 2014, where thousands of people had died. I had always thought that our governments should be doing more to help the people on these boats.

In 2015, I made my first trip to the Calais 'Jungle', where thousands of people were camped in horrendous conditions. I approached it with an open mind, knowing that I really didn't understand the complexities of the situation. Some people were saying that if we helped them there, then 'more would come'. They said not to encourage them, but I always felt that was a horrible point to make. You aren't helping people cross our border by giving them a coat; you're just keeping them warm. There has never been anything wrong with giving food to someone who is hungry or a blanket to someone who will sleep in a tent at night. That's just human decency and if anything, it's not enough.

Hopes and Dreams

When I arrived in the Calais 'Jungle', I met my first refugee. I was the one who was intimidated, having planned for an escape with my van if things had gone wrong. I guess that all my fears had been manufactured by the press, and a natural human tendency to be suspicious. It's those same fears that grip so many people in my country, which seems obsessed with 'illegal immigrants'. Amer was lovely. He has a contagious smile and instantly welcomed me into his ramshackle wooden home. He is from South Sudan and told me how soldiers had rounded up families in the Nuba Mountains, raping the women and taking the boys as child soldiers. He had escaped and made it all the way to northern France, where he sat in front of me. His only possessions were laid out in this shack, and here he was, offering me food and drink to make me feel welcome. I learned there and then that any judgements of mine were meaningless.

After this experience, I returned several times to northern France, taking coats, shoes, tents, blankets, food and whatever I could to help them. Nobody can ever explain to me that helping another human is a bad thing. After a while, I started working with the sea rescue teams, first in Lesvos and then out in the Central Mediterranean Sea. I've been part of the rescue of thousands of people. I have lost count of the numbers of bodies that I've seen: poor people trying to make it to European soil. Each one of them has a story, and like me, you, Doro, or anyone, their lives are important. There is no justification at all for our governments to simply allow them to drown. I'm horrified when people explain these drownings away with throwaway statements, blaming them for their own deaths, and trying to instil fear into other people of cultural and religious differences.

It is sometimes said that religion is the root cause of all

197

wars, but I've always thought that's a bit of a cop-out. Religion has just been the tool that greedy men have used to take what they want and have the power that they crave. The crux of every religion just tells us to love. To love thy neighbour – how easily has that been forgotten in this 'Christian' country? Our borders aren't of religion, they're either geographical or man-made, and wherever there is a border, people die. I feel that everything that we have is just borrowed, from the ground we walk on, to the air that we breathe. We can't take anything with us when we're gone, and we will have to give it all back. Who do we think we are to not allow other people to share in our fortunate opportunities? These arbitrary lines on a map, to me, they're meaningless.

So what do I think about whether Doro or anyone else is a refugee or an economic migrant? My view is that all opinions are irrelevant to someone drowning in the sea – we should help them. That's all. What do I think about someone who is cold, on the streets of Paris or in a tent in Lesvos? All opinions are irrelevant while people have to survive like this – we should help them. Why do we feel that we have to make these judgements and distinctions? A friend of mine who I met at a Fire Brigades Union conference says that his mother told him, 'You should never look down on someone, unless it is to give them a hand to help them up.' I like that.

I dream of a world where anyone can move anywhere. Where we live without fear or judgements, and we simply help each other where we can. Where if someone is without food, others will help them and if they need shelter, then no questions are asked. I just want to live in a kind world. I passionately believe that you have to create the world that you want to live in around you. Nothing will change unless people make it happen, so I want to live those changes. That's why I'll continue helping people at sea or sleeping rough on our streets – I want to be the change that I want to see in the world. The world around you can be influenced by what you want it to be. Live with kindness and kindness will follow you too.

I was interested to know what Doro's dreams were.

So for me, my dream is first to help my mom and to give my children better education. And to know my son. I have never seen him in my life. I wish one day that I will go back home. If it is possible. I wish to see my family in front of me. That will be all the happiness that I need. In Europe I want to work and maybe, if I get chance, I could bring my family to be with me. And to show a better way for my children, so that they never have to suffer like I have suffered. I don't want anybody in the world to get the same experience, the same sufferance as me, because I experienced it and I know how it is when they say you are going to suffer. Nobody should laugh at those words because me, I suffered.

My dream is to organise an association to help people who have lost hope. Like in Libya there are some people who have gone mad. But they are not really mad. Do you know what makes them mad? What they see! They see more dead bodies than they should see in their lives. They see people shooting each other. They see people taking knives and killing people. They experience prison and never come out. In Libya, where I was living, there are plenty of people who are mad. My dream is just to organise an association, and to come to take them to their parents. Because that would be happiness for their parents. I want to take them home because I know the suffering of the mothers. Our mothers cry every day to see their sons, and they don't know which condition their sons are living in Libya. They are not in contact with their sons.

I was doing plenty things for those people. I used to call them and sit down with them. Give them food and chat with them. They don't take baths or change their clothes. But their madness is not a real madness, it is what they see in the life that makes them mad. Their parents need to see them. Like I was talking to one mom in Zuwara. Her child had been shot in the leg. He was a Cameroon boy. I left him in Libya because I didn't have the power to help him. I directed him to the Red Cross to deport him to his own country. He was in the Red Cross for some weeks, and he ran from them, because he said that there was no good food and that he was sad. He came back to Bangala house. Before I left him, he finally gave me his parents' number. When I called his mom, she was crying, like every mom. Plenty moms are crying, and their sons are alive. All the rest of the young guys and women. I want to help people who are in Libya and hurting in the desert to go back to the motherland.

For me, God put me on this journey to learn and to have mercy because I know what's going on. It's not easy. If you go Agadez [in Niger], Brendan, you will cry. You will cry not because they suffer, but because they are hungry. They don't have anything to eat. It would make you cry. And they don't have anywhere for them to find work. And you will see a tough guy, he will go slim. Because unless people send him money, he cannot go forward, he cannot go back. He cannot even have something to eat. The only thing they have is to sit down and beg. It's sad.

Once like in Gambia, my uncle called me. He said he got one son who wants to make the journey and follow your footsteps to Europe. I said to him, 'If you really know how much you suffer to get your son back, he will not go. Some people they are finding their sons and they can't get them back. So if you like your son, just don't try it, to push him to that journey, because he is going to hell. He's not going to go and make it for you. He's going to die.'

It's often the parents that make people make this journey. Like me, I see it one day. I was sitting by my door, getting ready to go to work with friends. One woman was passing and saw that her son was sitting with us. She stood in front of us. She said to him, 'What are you doing here?' He said that he had come to see his friends: 'When you are here you don't get work, you don't get nothing to do. Early in the morning you come and see your friends. Your friends are following the journey and make it to Europe. They build houses for their mom and driving better cars. It's better than when you go to your father and ask for small money. Are you a man? Follow the journey.' And that time, I didn't know the journey. If I had known, I would just explain to the mom: 'Don't push your son to hell. Just believe in God and leave your son. Maybe he will make it in his own country. It is better than to go and suffer.'

My mom did not force me to take the journey, but my friends had this pressure from their parents. I will never push anybody of my friends to make this journey, because I know this journey and I know the suffering of this journey. In West Africa, plenty of boys are supported on this journey by their parents. When they fall into a problem, or they fall into the hell, or they fall into the water and die, their moms start to cry, 'I lose my son.' And before you cried to say I lost my son, you should stay with your son. Stay and give

him a better education and job. He can make it every time.
Everybody can make it where you are. When you get
hope to make it. It's what I experienced in this journey. But
before I started this journey, I thought that if I didn't, I
would never make it. That's a lie.

Some people can make it where you are. But for me,
our parents are our parents, but some of the words of our
parents, we shouldn't follow them. Because you can follow your parents' words, but when you fall into big
problems, your mom cannot help you. Your father cannot
help you. You yourself cannot help you. Only money. And
if your parents can't get the money, you're going to die! It
is a bad experience for African parents to push their children into the fire, into the hell. To push their children to
go to Europe by the sea. It is not a good experience for us.
And plenty of people who are on this journey are not
dying at home.

In West Africa, we are like a family. If I don't have food
one day, I go to my family's house, or my friend's house.
They suffer because of materials. No better houses, clothes,
cars. But it is not like in Libya. The only thing I want to say
is to the parents of Africa. I want to invite myself to the TV
stations and talk to the families. Let them try an association and try to get their children home. There are plenty
of people who think their children are dead, but there is no
communication. They are just mad. Some people are in
Libya and they just want to come out, but there is no way.
You cannot cross that desert again. You cannot go back.
The only way is to enter Tunisia. And to enter Tunisia, you
will walk. You have to be trafficked. Libyan people will
catch you when you try to make that journey and they will
traffic you. Libya is that. They don't need you, but they

don't want you to leave. They want to exploit you like a slave. Can I ask: which time slavery will finish in this world? Never! Slavery will still continue.

In my family, they know. Nobody from my cousins or children or anybody will try to make this journey while I am alive. I can't stand for that. If I can help them stay in their own countries, with a business or anything like that, I would like to help them. But if they still want to come, I can give them advice. And if they listen it will be good for them. I hope all of my family will not follow me. All of them know what happened to me. They all thought that I was dead. Nobody expected me to be alive. So anybody that talks with me will believe me, because I saw it. And I don't know how to lie. I just talked with what I see.

Thanks, Doro. Shall we finish there?

I just want to say before you stop: God bless Sea-Watch, and God bless you and all your family and all our friends. And thank you Sea-Watch. Yeah man!

Acknowledgements

Doro
I would like to thank the following people: my wife, Awa Faty, and my children, Ousmane and Kadiatou, for always loving me; Catherine and Susan for helping me after I arrived in France; Brendan for helping me tell my story; and all the people at Sea-Watch for rescuing me and all the rescues. I would like to thank everyone who gave support to this book.

Brendan
I would like to thank the following people, without whom this book would not have made it to print.

Doro: your courage and wisdom inspire me all the time. How brave you have been to retell such horror, all so that others don't follow in your footsteps. Your care for others is truly magnificent. You are a tribute to all of your family and friends, The Gambia and refugees throughout the world. It has been an honour to work with you to create this book, and I feel privileged that you wanted me to help you do it.

A few people have been instrumental in making the book happen. Most notably Anna Hickman, who spent hours reading, advising, correcting, rereading and supporting me in getting the initial manuscript to a stage where it could be brought to publishers for consideration. Anna, you gave so much of your time for free, and Doro and I are both incredibly grateful.

Jaz O'Hara is a constant supporter of refugees and this project, sharing content and advising throughout; importantly, connecting Anna to the project, knowing that she would make things work. Clare Moseley has been a supporter of Doro and this project, right from his arrival in Europe, funding my trip to France, where the bulk of the interviews occurred. You helped bring attention to the project, getting people to support it through Care4Calais. Doro and I are really grateful for your efforts.

Bronwen Griff, who read the initial transcriptions of the interview, and then gave her time to advise. It is because of you that the book uses Doro's voice throughout, with very limited changes. Your advice in the early stages of formulating how we would get this to paper was much needed at the time. You then helped with the first edits, along with Caroline Gregory and Frances George (may you rest in peace), who both also deserve special recognition for their reading, support and edits.

John Borton, Sue Clayton, Jayne Melland, Haidi Sadik, Berenice Gaudin and Lorenzo Bagnoli all lent their expertise in their individual areas to ensure that the book worked. Fact-checking, giving regional advice (Gambia and Libya) and legal advice were all important areas to get right, and I am grateful for your support in these key areas.

I would like to thank all at Unbound for believing in and supporting the project, and for all the work that you have done to get this from being a concept into being an actual book, including Katy Guest, Rachael Kerr, Cassie Waters, Tamsin Shelton, Lisa Fiske, Kate Quarry, Imogen Denny, Sophie Griffiths and Mark Ecob. There are so many people behind the scenes: you know who you are, and we are grateful.

Catherine Berthon, I asked you to look after Doro, to take care of him and give him all the support that he needed on his arrival and in his initial solitude in France. You kept him as safe as you could, kept your word, and more. Thank you for all that you did for Doro and continue to do for others.

I would like to thank my friends and family for helping me through some really difficult moments as this project reached its final stages. George Woodhouse and Jennifer Woodhouse (may you rest in peace) always understood the importance of the writing of this and gave so much encouragement. When Jennifer died, my friends and family stood me back on my feet. For that, I have no words that could do justice to their support.

Harriet, you are the most selfless and loving person that I have ever met. Thank you for surrounding me in your love and for helping me write again. To my parents, John and Veronica, and to my brother John, I want to thank you for your forever support – it means everything. George, you make me want to wake up every day: together we can face anything.

To all at Sea-Watch for continuing the rescues, you all

know the importance of this. Being part of Sea-Watch, you are part of Doro's journey too. His is one story of the thousands that we have collectively brought to safety. Never stop believing!

To all in the Fire Brigades Union, who have always had my back, from writing to the Foreign Secretary to demand our release when Doro and I were on the ship together, to supporting the project once the initial manuscript was written, to pledging support in such incredible numbers. Many of your names are in the back of this book and I can't mention you all, but most notably, Adam Taylor, Ben Selby, Matt Wrack, Tam McFarlane, Riccardo la Torre, Ian Murray and Clare Hudson.

There have been a lot of other people who supported, encouraged and give little bits of advice along the way that I haven't mentioned, so if I forgot to mention you – sorry and thanks.

This book would simply not have been printed without people believing in the project, sharing the supporters' page and pledging financial support. I am really grateful. Thank you all!

A Note on the Authors

Doro Goumãñęh is a former fisherman from The Gambia who now lives in France as a refugee. He speaks many languages and is currently working as an electrician.

Brendan Woodhouse is a former British Army combat medic, with twenty years' experience as a firefighter in the UK. Brendan has been involved in the search and rescue of over 8,000 refugees since the start of 2015, mainly with Sea-Watch.

Unbound is the world's first crowdfunding publisher, established in 2011.

We believe that wonderful things can happen when you clear a path for people who share a passion. That's why we've built a platform that brings together readers and authors to crowdfund books they believe in – and give fresh ideas that don't fit the traditional mould the chance they deserve.

This book is in your hands because readers made it possible. Everyone who pledged their support is listed below. Join them by visiting unbound.com and supporting a book today.

Matthias Abele
Aliya Abidi
Kylie Ackers
Helen Adams
Keith Adsley
Alcindo
Cristina Alcov
Yva Alexandrova
Rick Allain
Diana Allen
Katrina Allen
Hazel Allister

Jord An
Neil Anderson
Jessica Andersson
Debbie Andrews
Jonathan Angell
Anka
Arddun Arwyn
Luisa Asue
Athens Volunteers
    Information &
    Coordination Group
Laura Atherton Walker

Victoria Attwooll
Ali Bailey
Anne Baker
Rachel Baker
Yasmin Bandali
Stephanie Banks
Rachel Bannister
Linda Bargate
Kathy Barnby
Teresa Batchelor
Nadia Batool
Natalia Battistini
Amber Bauer
Guy Beards
Sally Beazley
Christine Beckett
Alice Beckett-McGahon
David Beckler
Sazzer Bee
Antonia Bennett
Jeane Benny
Hannah Benson
Frances Bernstein
Sarah Berry
Tess Berry-Hart
Catherine Berthon
Neil Bevan
Rosie Birmingham
Emily Birrell
Claire Bishop
Sophie Bluestone
Laura Bolton

Stephen Bond
Giuseppe Borello TTT
Lesley Boulton
Julie Bourdin
Georgina Bowker Heighes
Steph Bown
Jean Boyne
Phil Brachi
Carly Bradbury
Annie Bradley
Vanessa Braga Evans
Ariana Brahaj
Frances Brain
Mary Brandon
Jessica Breakey
Brian Brennan
Tamsyn Brewster
Ela Bri
Jenny Bridgeman
Chris Brodie
Olive Brodie-Stuart
Nina Bromham
Anna Brown
Gavin Brown
Brian Browne
Katrin Glatz Brubakk
Knut Bry
Richard Buckwell
Christina Burden
Mike Burgess
Ann Burnett
Silke Busch

Camilla Bushill
Kath Bushnell
Sayhra Butt
Mireille Cagnol
Harriet Camille-Todd
Mairead Canavan
Katrine Carlsson
Patric Carlsson
Richenda Carlton
Catherine Carpenter
Andrea Carr
Sarah Carré, The People
  and Planet Company
Dan Carter
Patti Carter Nicholson
Fiona Cartmell
Angharad Cartwright
Gaby Casemore
Victoria Casey
Julia Cave
Ilya Cereso
Gill Chadwick
Sara Chandler
Bridget Chapman
Miri Christie-Mann
Angus Clark
Hannah Clarke
Russell Cleirich
Helen Cliff
John Clifton
Sandy Clubley
Anna Clyne

Dani Cobb
Kate Cocker
Stephan Collishaw
Andrea Coluccio
Melissa Connolly
Elizabeth Coombes
Esther Coren
Emily Corker
Steven Corrigan
Sophie Cottis-Allan
Hannah Coulman
Caitlin Cowan
Ben Cowles
Chris Cox
Heaven Crawley
Sally Croft Kay
Rebecca Crofton
Clare Crombie
Claire Crook
Paulette Crooke
John Crosby
Gabrielle Crossley
Margaret Crow
Rosa Crowley-Bennett
Nicola Cui
Saya Cullinan
Natalie Czaban
Joanna Czechowska
Antonia Dagorova
Joanna Daisley
Rod Darby
Anne Darcy

Laurie Davidson

Pauline Davidson

Elizabeth Eva Seren Davies

Lois Davies

Robert Davies

Samantha Davies

Sue Davies

Zoe Davis

Amanda Dawson

Kate Dawson

Catarina de Almeida

Irene De Bartolo

Matteo de Bellis

Jan de Jager

Tarciane de Oliveira
Almeida

Mélanie Declercq

Anne Dekker

Rachel Delacy-Hancock

Pam Delargy

Rachel Delourme

Curtis Delyn

Asli Demirel

Ciara Devlin

Annie Dew

Katherine Yvonne Dickson

Jo Doheny

Christine Dolan

Anne Doran

Andrew Draper

Hayley Dreamsmasher

Liza Dresner

Rose Drew

Mélanie Duflo

Orlaith Durcan

Caitlin Durnbaugh

Selma Dzafic

Ellie E

Robert Eardley

Claire Earl

Jillian Edelstein

Nettie Edmondson

Angharad Edmunds

Jemima Edwards

Batten Ellie

Nicki Ellis

Jacqui Elston-Rigby

Jörg Enderlein

Suzy Ensor

Olivia Errey

Caroll Esterhuizen

Kelsey Esteves

Claire Evans

Petra Evison

Holly Exley

Dee Fairchild

Pippa J Fairhead

Rachel Faraday

Natalie Faria-Vare

Gemma Fawcett-Wilson

Jackie Fearnley

Alicia Felling

Sebastian Felling

Luiza Fernandes

Patric ffrench Devitt
Patricia Fiddian
Toni Fifield
Becky Fincham
Fire Brigades Union
Zoe Fishel
Sarah Fisher
Fishhead
Nicola Flint
Gina Flynn
Cheryl Forshaw
Stephen Foster
Ash Fox
Richard Fox
Laurens Francis
Melanie Francis
Chloé François-Nienaber
Dalia Frantz
Claire Fraser
Guenter Fritz
Valerie Fry
Victoria Fullard
Dawn Fuller
Janet Fuller
Carla Fyfe
Anne Gadsden
Rebecca Gaon
Nancy Garcia
Susan Gardner
Claire Gautam
Bronwyn Gavine
Sue Geary

Hannah Gee
Cathelijne Geuze
Chris Gibbon
Laura Gibbs
Jay Ginn
Drew Ginsburg
Kerry Gird
Shirley Godwin
Alex Godwin-Brown
Rebecca Goodall
Zoe Goode
Lavinia Gordon
Claire Govender
Merel Graeve
Karen Graham
Moira Grandon-Moran
Rosa Granero
Frances Gray
Mary Gray
Kate Gray United
    Reformed Church
Griffin Greenaway
Beau Jessica
    Greenwood-Wileman
Caroline Gregory
Sarah Grey
Sonhild Grey
Olivia Grez Haniewicz
Stephen Grice
Becky Gries
Bronwen Griffiths
Catherine Griffiths

Supporters

Cerith Griffiths
David Grimley
Elisa Groenendijk
Madelena Grossmann
Katy Guest
Nellie-Anne Guijt
Melanie Guilfoyle
Girish Gupta
Sheilagh Guthrie
Alice Guy
Angela Haddon
Jacqueline Hadj Hamou
Katherine Haggan
Geoffrey Hale
Lizzie Hall
Wendy Hall
Gabriella, Michelle and
    Leon Hallmark
Murray Hallwood
Esther Hamill
Val Hampshire
Susie Hanley
Rachel Harford
Jody Harris
Maddie Harris
Sara Harris
Imelda Harrison
Nicola Harrison
Rachel Hattingh
Sally Hayden
Liz Hayes
Ayesha Heaton

Rachel Henderson
Clare Hennessy
Laurel Henry
Jane Henson
Andy Hersham
Lorna Hibbert
Kathryn Hick
Lesley Hick
Lesley Hill
Vanessa Hiller
Cath Hollywell
June Holmes
Nonie Horsman
Emma-Lyn Horvath
Ann Howard
Steve Howse
Sanaa Htn
Christine Huckstepp
Cassie Hudson
Clare Hudson
Jade Hughes
Sarah Hunak
Jesse Huppenbauer
Laura Hussey
Deborah Hyde
Laura Hyland
Angela & Andrew Hynd
Rossella Icardi
Amna Idries
Jill Ingham
Jim Innes
Sophie Ireland

Angie Jackson
Damian Jackson
Fay Jackson
Gill Jackson
Kevyn Jalone
Elizabeth James
Linda James
Samantha Jane
Rebecca Jasper
Chaturini Jayasuriya
Moyra Jean
Amy Jefferies
Kristal Jenks
Jane Jermyn
Adams Jill
jonandboots
Elise Jones
Katy Jones
Sheila Jones
Simon Jones
Susan Jones
Khandiz Joni
Annette Jonker
Claire Judge
Adam Jung
Beth K
Heba Kadous
Petya Kalinova
Jasmine Kay-Moyle
Penelope Kaye
KDRSG
Diane Kearton

Felicity Kelly
Lucy Kelly
Niamh Kelly
Suzanne Kelly
Stacey Kemp
Val Kemp
Eric Kempson
Anne Kiely
Emma Kiely
Dan Kieran
Sally Kincaid
Rob King
Randi Kinman
Claire Kirby
Eleanor Kirby
Thorsten Kliefoth
Johanneke Kodde
Fiona Kolontari
Evgenia Kroz
Doug Kuntz
Myria Kyriacou
Riccardo la Torre
Shirley Lackner
Ann Jane Laemmer
Linsey Laidlaw
Carie Lainchbury
Pam Lake
Rob Lake
Gail Lamb
Mark Lampert
Jane Lancashire
Isabel Lancaster

Rachel Lasserson
Katy Last
Linda Lawton
Jess Layton
Dea Le Bargy
Brian Le Marquand
Rachel Le Mesurier
Sierra Leash
Rebecca Lee
James Leslie
Louise LeVell
Micky LeVoguer
Chloe Lewington
Rothstein Lisa
Tim Lloyd
Samantha Logan-Hochadel
Elizabeth Long
Jane Longshaw
Alexandra Lopez
Linda Lovelock
Aaron Lowe
Samantha Lowe
Pauline Lowrie
Lori DeSain Lozano
Carol Lyon
Kate Lyons
Jerome Maas
Sue MacFarlane
Rebecca MacLellan
Amy Maguire
Marji Mansfield
Michèle Marconi

Mario Marcoz
Vanessa Marjoribanks
Lucy Marshall
Natalie Martin
Polly Martin
Martina
Cameron Matthews
Elise Maurel
Evan May
Ellen McArthur
Angela Mccool
Fiona McDaid
Angela McDermott-Roe
Patricia McGarry
Bibi McGee
Christine McGinn
Clara McGrane
Laura McMahon
Emma McNamara
Ros Meadow
David Quinney Mee
Lucia Mee - Kindred spirits
Ged Meechan
Leila Meechan
Jayne Melland
Danielle Mercey
Lisa Merker
Sajad Merzayi
Paula Mesurera
Sumaia Migou
Netty Miles
Richard Miller

Nicola Milner
Alyssa Mireles
Charmaine Mirza
John Mitchinson
Tara Montane
Michelle Moore
Janet Moran
Rita Moreira da Silva
Jennifer Morice
Andrew Moss
Sally Moss
Debbie Mossman
Kim Mottier
Gillian Moyes
Souad Msallem
Cath Muldowney
Jessica Mumford
Nicola Jane Munro
Hannah Murden-Landman
Elaine Murray
Karen Murray
Rachel Murray
N. Derbyshire Stand up to
  Racism
Michael Nangalia
Carlo Navato
Glenys Newton
Laura Nixon
Gemma Noi
Katie Nokes
Erika Norrie
Terry Norwick

Julia Nye
Mairin O Faolain
Annabelle Julie O'Connell
Jenny O'Gorman
Simon O'Hara
Julie O'Hearn
Lorraine O'Sullivan
Tarryn Oberholzer
Gail Obrien
Elaine Ofori
Frances ONeill
Charlenne Ordonez
Elaine Ormiston
Jane Owen
Tim Owen
P.Bon
Karen Paalman
Veronika Pachala
Jes Padgett
Lucas Paeth
Annie Page
Rosemary Paisley
Giulia Pallanca
Marian Pallister
Steph Parker
Kelly Parkhouse
Rebecca Parry
Suzanne Partridge
Ruth Paskins
Jo Patel
Priyal Patel
Caroline Patterson

Supporters

Jane Paul
Vivienne Pay
Angela Pearce
Ruth Penfold
Penny and Kevin
Timothy Perkins
Catherine Perque
Bill Perry
Kathryn Perry
Angela Pert
Anneke Phillips
Joan Pidgeon
Anrike Piel
Felicity Pike
Grace Plahe
PlayFair PlayFair
Frances Plowden
Justin Pollard
Taz Pollard
Katie Pollitt
Míyka Porcelli
Adrian Pourviseh
Rosemary Power
Ruth Pownall
Carrie Price
Caroline Pritchard
Fi Pugh
Antonieta Puig-Maurici
Joanna Quinlan
Raagib Quraishi
Pete Radcliff
Dominique Rade

Kathryn Radley
Cat Radnor
Karam Radwan
Micha Ramsay
Sara Ramsey
Smaira Rana
Steve Rawcliffe
Lynn Rawson
Laura Read
Marc Redford
Nicola Redmond
Joe Redston
Felicity Reed
Mandy Reeman-Clark
Louise Regan
Barbara Reid
Moira Reid
Paula Reidy
Paula Render
Julia Retkova
Dan Revill
Nicholas Rhodes
Kathy Richardson
Davina Ridley
Ana Riella
Alyx Rigney
Rebecca Robinson
Sarah Robinson
Ms Jane Robson
Johann Roden
Andrew Rogers
Claire Rogerson

Louise Rolfe
Giulia Rompel
Emma Rose
Geraldine Rose
Harriet Rose
Sue Ross
Lis Royston-Bishop
Robert Russell
Julie Ryder
Maddy Salisbury
Holligan Sally
Lauren Sanchez
Sarah Sanders
Aurora Santin
Bernice Sargent
Jo Saunders
Lynne Scannell
Leslie Meral Schick
Jenny Scott
Nancy Seager
Kristen Seeley
Ben Selby - FBU
Annie Shaffer
Allison Sharma
Ashu Sharma
Gavin Sharp
Dan Shaw
Jen Shaw-Sweet
Rosie Shearer
Lisa Shepherd
Joe Short
Ylan Shupilov

Andrea Shuttleworth
Paula Siddall
Emma Simpson
Matthew Simpson
Lenke Slegers
Heidi Sleiman
Pamela Sloan
Amy Smallman
Katy Smart
Della Smith
Kerry Smith
Martyn Smith
Sandra Smith
Matt Snellin
Ben Solanky
Hanna Solman
Joe Solo
Carol Southgate
Dannie Sowden
Ilaria Spelta
Catherine Spencer
Pauline PB Spencer
Angus Sproul
Marianne Stack
Sally Standart
Katjusa Stanek
Luděk Stavinoha
Viktor Steiner
Patricia Stephenson
Cooke Steve
Evelyn Stevens
Sheena Stewart

Supporters

Beth Strachan
Mary Stretch
Marsha Sutcliffe
Jon Svikis
Nicola Swain
Magdalena Szlenkier
Adam Taylor
Sarah Taylor
Soraya Tayob
Alison Terry-Evans
Theboyrickyg
Elizabeth Thomas
Susan Thornton
Mats Thünemann
Janet Tighe
Karen Tinsley
Kev Titterton
C A Todd
Sarah Tolley
Sarah Tollison
Jennie Tomlinson
Christine Toth
Ben Traynor
Caroline Tredget
Lauren Tree
Helen Tremeer
Wren Trevisan
Natalie Trotter-King
Hannah Tuck
Sarah Tunnicliffe
Jessica Twitchin
Gina Ty-Wharton

Beth Tysdal
Ira Udaskin
Shona Sara Heather Ure
Anna Uwins
Simone van den Akker
Anna Van Der Poorten
Nynke van Dijck
Erika Van Houweninge
Saskia van Manen
Teresa VanLoey
Ambroise Vardon
Isabel Villena Toledo
James Vinciguerra
Hannah Vitacolonna
Karin Volkner
Karl Wager
sharon walia
Lee Walker
Linda Walker
Lorna Walker
Lynne Walker
Susan Walker
Caroline Walton
Abigail Ward
Judith-Ann Wardlaw
Elfrieda Waren
Lilly Warren
Rabbi Lee Wax
Clare Webster
Robert Webster-Shaw
Steve Weir
Em Weirdigan

Maggie Weirdigan
Jordan Zoe Wellard
Tetske Welling
Joanne Welsh
John West
Sarah Westcott
Adam Westerink
Rosie Whelan
Keith White
Kate Whiting
Yvonne Williams
Barbara Wilson
Jacquie Wilson
Nancy Wilson Fulton
Sandra Witt
Chloe Wolfe
Amy Wood
Joshua Wood

Steve Woodger
Michael Woodhouse
Veronica Woodhouse
John Woodhouse, dialogue
Laura Woodward
Sam Woolliss
Angelita Woosnam
Elizabeth Worsley
Larry Wright
Lindsay Wright
Danielle Wyatt
Ellie Wyatt
Abra Wynn
Michelle Yanefski
Yun Yeung
Heather Young
Davinder Youngs
Anita Zwicky